Gir

Girl to Girl

Finding Our Voices

Karen Casey

HAZELDEN®
INFORMATION & EDUCATIONAL SERVICES

Hazelden
Center City, Minnesota 55012-0176

1-800-328-0094
1-651-213-4590 (Fax)
www.hazelden.org

Library of Congress Cataloging-in-Publication Data

Casey, Karen.
Girl to girl : finding our voices / Karen Casey.
p. cm.
Includes index.
ISBN 1-56838-372-X
1. Teenage girls. 2. Teenage girls—Conduct of life.
3. Devotional calendars. 4. Affirmations.

HQ798 .C276 2000
305.235—dc21 99-086566

04 03 02 01 00 6 5 4 3 2 1

Cover design by Mary Brucken
Cover illustration by Kelly Stribling Sutherland
Interior illustrations by Patrice Barton
Interior design by Nora Koch/Gravel Pit Publications
Typesetting by Stanton Publication Services, Inc.

Acknowledgments

My journey as a writer has been increasingly rewarding. Even though I had never set out to be one, I cannot imagine a more wonderful way to have spent the past few years of my life. Having a husband like Joe has made my "labor of love" quite exciting, really. He has always been close by, supporting my efforts and helping me laugh my way through the rough parts. A better partnership seems inconceivable.

Patricia Hoolihan is a wonderful editor. She massaged the words and the message, making the book far more readable. And she has a sensitive ear and a loving spirit; both were needed in this pursuit. Thank you, Patricia.

To Bette Nowacki and Rebecca Post, I offer my heartfelt thanks. Each of you came through in an invaluable way. The book became a reality because of your help.

And to Hazelden, I say thanks once again. You have helped so many in so many ways. I am grateful that I have been part of the publishing "family" for nearly two decades.

Last, but definitely not least, I thank all my friends in recovery. Were it not for you, I would not have survived to write this or any other book. I owe you guys my life.

A Note to Parents

I remember vividly my own troubled youth. I seldom had the confidence and certainly never the wisdom to make very intelligent choices for my life. I was easily led astray and constantly fearful that I didn't fit in, wasn't popular enough or smart enough, and absolutely not cute enough. I wore thick glasses and had long, skinny legs and arms.

There were so many things I needed to talk over with a parent or teacher, but never did. I simply bumbled my way along, never receiving or seeking the guidance that might have helped me on my journey. I am assuming that many young girls today struggle as I struggled. And I am also assuming that you might know one of them. This book is for her. And it's a book that you can give her, along with your willingness to talk over any of the selections that strike her fancy, or yours.

I know how busy you are as parents. And I know how frequently you wish you had the time to listen more intently to a daughter when it seems a problem is troubling her. It is my hope that this book will ease your way. The many ideas expressed here, in language that will resonate with your daughter, should open the door to having the many conversations that both of you want but simply haven't taken the time for. On any single day, she can read for you or share with you what the message is. And the time will be ripe for a deeper discussion of that message.

I hope you enjoy this book together. I hope it draws you closer, and I hope it prepares her for the journey she deserves, one day at a time.

Dear Reader,

Hi. I am so glad you have picked up this book to read. I think I have a lot of messages that will help you on a day-to-day basis. That's the best way to read the book. In the morning before going to school, take five minutes or so to read the page for the day. If there is something you think your mom or dad might like to talk about, remember to read it to them later in the day. And then talk. Nobody talks as much as they should. Too many of us, kids as well as adults, walk around with problems on our minds, and we fail to ask our friends or the adults who care about us to give us some guidance.

One thing that I want you to know is that when I was your age I had a lot of worries. I worried that I wasn't popular enough, that I wasn't as cute as many of my friends, that I was too skinny and not very smart. I worried about being left out when friends got together. It seems, when I think back, that my life as a young girl wasn't all that happy. My constant worrying kept me from enjoying a lot of the activities that I was involved in. I failed to talk to my parents or the school guidance counselors, and I am sure that if I had, they would have offered help.

I don't want you to struggle the way I did. That's why I have written this book. I think too many young girls have fears they could be free of if only they talked them over with someone. I believe this book will help you find a way to talk things over. It might also help you be able to just let go of many of the problems that seem to wait for you while you sleep. I have learned that one of the best ways of getting over a problem or being free from worry is to ask God to handle the situation. Often I write God a note and then put it in a safe place for a few days. And guess what—when I read the note a few days later, I usually discover that the problem has been solved. You can do this exercise regardless of how old you are. You might even share the idea with a parent.

I am really glad you are reading this book. I like making new friends and I would love to hear from you. If you have an idea you would like to share with me or want to tell me how you were specifically helped by something you read here, please write to me, Karen Casey, at Hazelden Information and Educational Services, P.O. Box 176, Center City, MN 55012.

I am looking forward to our new friendship.

Yours truly,
Karen Casey

January

Happiness can happen.

Being happy is up to each one of us. Abraham Lincoln supposedly said, "We are as happy as we make up our minds to be." My teacher said she didn't know if he really said it, but it is a good philosophy to live by anyway, because it means we can be happy in almost any circumstance.

I've been thinking about this idea and I like it. For instance, if it rains when I had planned on going to the state fair, I can go to the movies instead. Or if I ask Shelly to sleep over and she says no, I can ask Leah. Maybe it isn't easy to be happy with a disappointment, but it can be done.

Today will be a good day to start being in charge of my happiness.

January 2

And what a delight it is to make friends with someone you have despised.

Colette

Showing my friends, especially Jessica, that I care about them is important. I used to hate Jessica. I'm not sure why, but I think it was because she had more friends than I had. She is probably the smartest girl in our class, and I envied her. When she and I had to do a project together in school, I found out that she's kind and a lot of fun. She seemed interested in me and asked me great questions about myself.

Now I really like to spend time with Jessica. I show it by waiting for her at her locker and sometimes by defending her to the other girls who still envy her.

My feelings toward others can change if I keep an open heart.

Wanting attention is a common trait.

I hate it when my friend Shannon gets so much attention from our science teacher. I know Mr. Lorentz thinks she is the smartest one in our class. I don't think so, though. If I had Dad at home to help me, I would be smarter in science, too, and I probably wouldn't care so much about the attention Mr. Lorentz gives Shannon. I wish my dad came to see me more often. I miss him so much.

I'm glad I have school to go to and a little brother, even though Tony gets into my favorite things. But even when people are around, I'm lonely some of the time. Mom says our hearts long for certain people and the way things used to be. I guess my heart longs for my dad to tuck me in at night, like he used to when I was younger.

If I feel lonely today, I will try making a new friend.

January 4

The crucial task . . . is balance.

Florida Scott Maxwell

Having fun is what being alive is partly about. Of course, there's work to be done, too. Maybe the best way to live is to make fun out of our work. That's what my dad does. He says that makes his life more balanced. He believes even kids need balance. All work and no play isn't good for anybody.

My mom keeps trying to teach me to do my homework and practice piano first and then play. I don't always want to, but when I'm done and free to play, that feels so good.

I can make room in my life for work (practice, studies, cleaning my room) and play.

Death comes to everything.

Our pet bird died the other day. Actually, it was kind of our fault. My sister, Sara, let it out of its cage before we all went to church. After we got home, we hurried to my grandmother's house for dinner and then went to a movie. By the time we got home we had forgotten about the bird. The next morning it wasn't in its cage, and then Sara remembered she had let it out. We looked everywhere for it. We found it dead on the steps to the basement.

We felt really sad. During breakfast we talked about death. Mom said getting used to having death visit our home was OK because everything dies eventually. I'm not crazy about that idea, but Mom said we should share our feelings and questions about death. She said we could be open and honest about our sadness.

I believe that my parents will help me with any problem, especially when I'm feeling sad.

January 6

Generosity can be many things.

Sharing my stuff with friends is one way of being generous. We talk about sharing quite often in school. It isn't always easy to be generous with our things, but we can be generous with our attention, too. Amanda's mother says that every time we are generous in even a small way, something good comes back to us.

A couple of weeks ago I called Kate a lot to see how she was doing. She was upset because her brother was fighting with her dad every day. Then when I was feeling bad because I didn't pass my skating test, she called to make sure I was OK. Maybe this is what Amanda's mother is talking about.

I will consider being generous with my thoughts or my attention at school today.

Words are more powerful
than perhaps anyone suspects.

May Sarton

My grandmother says we often say mean things to the people who are closest to us. For example, I yelled at my little brother and called him stupid for knocking my glass of milk over at the dinner table. He started to cry. Grandma said my words were cruel.

She reminded me of how long I felt sad and angry when my former best friend, Tammy, uninvited me to her birthday party. She told all of the kids that I had stolen her homework. That wasn't true, and her mean words about me hurt. I was afraid everyone was going to drop me as a friend.

I will try to consider my words before I say them today. Hurting others is wrong.

January 8

Mistakes are not the end of the world,
but we could try harder.

Almost everyone in my room at school didn't do well on last Friday's big test. Miss Benson was pretty disgusted with our class. She had worked hard to help us learn all the states on the East Coast. During the practice test, I got twelve out of fifteen correct. Megan was the only one who got a perfect score on the actual test, though. She usually gets an A+ in every subject, and she doesn't seem to study any harder than the rest of us.

I hate to get bad grades. How do your parents react when you get bad grades? Perfection isn't easy. My dad says I can't expect to be perfect in most things, but I can concentrate, and then I won't make silly mistakes. Most of the mistakes I made on last Friday's test were silly. Being careful might change that.

I will go slower today when I do my schoolwork.
Silly mistakes can be avoided.

Compromise is a skill we will need for the rest of our lives.

Meeting someone halfway rather than fighting to get your way when playing a game with a friend is a good idea. My older brother says it's good practice for growing up. Adults have to compromise all the time if they want to make progress at work or in their relationships. Dad said he learned this from a counselor he and Mom went to when they were thinking about splitting up.

Compromise is an important idea to put to work in our lives. Last week I compromised with my sister Holly by agreeing to wash dishes if she would clean up our bedroom. We each did a job that we liked. Mom says compromise doesn't always happen that easily, but it does always prevent unnecessary arguments. Growing up means giving in once in a while. Practice makes us better at it.

I will no doubt have an opportunity to compromise with a classmate today. I will try to be the one to think of a way to agree.

January 10

*The bottom line is I am responsible
for my own well-being.*

Kathleen Andrus

Taking responsibility for whatever mistakes we make is hard. I am ashamed of some things I do. Last week I left the chocolate revel ice cream on the kitchen counter after scooping some out for myself, and it melted. It ran off the counter onto the kitchen floor. Boy, was my family mad. Dad had brought the ice cream home for our dessert, and I was the only one who got any.

Yesterday Mom locked her keys in the car when she went to the grocery store. We didn't have an extra set of keys because my dad was out of town. Mom paid a locksmith forty-five dollars to let her into the car. Taking responsibility for that mistake was embarrassing for her. Is there a way to avoid mistakes?

I will try to act responsibly today, and that includes trying to make up for any harm from my mistakes.

What does honesty mean to you?

I don't like to accept the blame for many things I do. Last night I left my bedroom window open and it rained in, getting my bed, my collection of dolls, and the floor wet. At first I pretended that someone else had opened the window. But it upset me to know that I was lying. I figured my mom knew I was lying, too. After all, who else could have opened my window? My little brother can't reach that high and my dad would have remembered to close it.

Making mistakes and admitting them is an important lesson in growing up. Just last week my teacher reminded us how important this is. Her example was the time Brenda said that she had turned her math homework in when she hadn't. Right after lunch, Brenda told the teacher she had lied. Mrs. Hadly praised Brenda for being honest. She didn't even give her detention for the lie she had told.

I can work on my honesty today. If at first I start to blame someone else for something I did or simply tell a little lie about something I'm embarrassed about, I will stop myself.

January 12

Grumbling is the death of love.
Marlene Dietrich

One of the most important and easiest decisions a person can make every day is to have a good attitude. Mr. Green, our music teacher, reminds us of this constantly. He says that when we're frowning while singing, our voices aren't pretty. My mother agrees. Sometimes she accuses me of getting up on the wrong side of the bed. What a funny saying. I always get up on the same side. The other side of my bed is up against the wall. I couldn't get up on that side even if I wanted to!

Mom and I looked up the word "attitude" in the dictionary yesterday. It says, "Attitude is a way of thinking or behaving." When I am pouting or yelling at my sister or picking on her, my attitude is bad. I don't like it when others are crabby toward me, either. Everybody can work on their attitude once in a while. Yesterday my dad reminded me that I could change my attitude quickly if I wanted to.

I would rather have a good attitude than a bad one. Nobody has much fun when I am in a bad mood. Especially me!

Prayer enlarges the heart.

Mother Teresa

Do you pray before going to sleep at night? I do except when a girlfriend stays over. Then I feel embarrassed about saying my prayers, but I sometimes say them quietly if I have a worry on my mind. Maybe it would be a good idea to talk this over with my mother. I think she prays at night. I wonder if she gets embarrassed if my dad is listening.

Prayer is an important part of my family's life. Mom says it helps to take away her fear, especially when she's trying something new. She believes God is always willing to listen, and not just at night. She says that fear makes her world smaller and prayer helps open her heart to love the world and her place in it.

I will ask God about everything that troubles me today.
This will be my experiment for the day.

January 14

To each particular person the world speaks a different, particular word and calls for a different, particular response.

Mary McDermott Shideler

My grandmother says we are who we need to be, "warts and all." I am not always convinced I really need to be short and a little chubby, but it does make me conscious of how easily someone's feelings can be hurt when they are labeled "fat." Because I understand this, I can offer comfort to Barbara, who gets teased a lot because she is the heaviest girl in the ninth grade.

My dad is good at making me laugh and helping me pull out of bad moods. My stepmom is comforting when I'm sick or feeling blue. I've noticed that if I want help planning a party, Sara is the one I can count on. Carmen's specialty is homework assignments. She has helped me many times when I got behind. It does seem that everyone has something special to offer.

My character traits offer me opportunities that are specific to me alone. That's a comforting idea.

Helping others never goes unnoticed.

One of the best gifts I can give someone is to offer to help. That's what my stepmom reminds me of at least once every day. I took her suggestion yesterday. I went over to Josh's house and offered to push his sister in her stroller. She giggled all the way around the block. Josh's mother was happy for the help, too. She said she got the kitchen floor mopped at last!

I think I'll offer to help my dad with something today. He seems so tired when he comes home from work. I wonder what he would like help doing? Maybe I can wash his car. I noticed that it was really dirty. His shop is a mess, too. If my bedroom looked anything like his shop, I'd be in trouble. I wonder if he wants my help?

There are many ways I can help others today.
I will offer my help to three people.

January 16

In every relationship, in every moment,
we teach either love or fear.

Marianne Williamson

Abby is always arguing with someone. At lunch yesterday she was yelling at Missy. I'm not sure what Missy had done, but she was crying. I felt sorry for her. It seems Abby is never having a good time. I hate to fight. It makes me jumpy inside.

I wonder why some kids fight so much. I've noticed that the same ones seem to do it all the time. Dad says that people who feel insecure and afraid fight as a cover-up because they don't really want others to know they feel that way. I wonder if Abby feels like others are better than her. Maybe that's why she's always picking fights. Maybe she needs more friends. Maybe she's going through a hard time and needs kindness from others.

I will try to be extra nice today to the person who keeps picking fights.

It always hurts to feel left out.

Everybody has hurt feelings sometimes. Brad sure acted hurt yesterday when the boys in his group didn't ask him to play kickball. He just walked off and sat by the school fence. I wonder why they left him out? He's the tallest in the group and I've seen him kick. He is really good!

I got my feelings hurt when I found out that Rachel had asked Teri and Sasha to her house for pizza and didn't ask me. My first thought was that Rachel didn't like me anymore. I wanted to ask her but I was afraid of what she might say. Mother said she probably didn't have room for one more and that perhaps I would be included next time. I hope she's right. Do you ever get left out of a friend's plans? How do you feel when it happens?

If I get left out of a plan today, I will try to remember that it's not so important to be included every time.

January 18

My life is blessed.
I have riches beyond belief.

Joan Rohde

When my grandmother is feeling sad, she writes down the things that make her happy. This helps her remember to focus on the good things in her life. That seems like a good idea to me.

Last week I was feeling sad because Tamara moved away. She has been my best friend since third grade. I like Sophie and Dana, too, but Tamara was my favorite friend. We even had the exact same dolls when we first met. The first couple of years of our friendship, we pretended we were mothers living next door to each other.

Maybe I should make a list of the things that make me happy. What could I put on it? The first thing on it might be that I'm lucky to have had a friend like Tamara, and when we get older we can visit each other.

I will start a list of the things that make me happy.

Confidence takes lots of practice.

What are your ideas about "confidence"? Miss Perez asked us about that yesterday in our English class. The short story we were reading was about a boy who was afraid he couldn't make it to the dentist by himself on the bus because he had just moved to a new city. His mother had given him a note explaining exactly what he should do, but he never got on the bus when it stopped at the corner because he was afraid. Miss Perez said he lacked confidence in himself. She had each of us write another ending for the story.

I was afraid of going into the dark basement when I was little. Maybe I was like Tim in our story, but I'm not afraid of going down into the basement anymore. I'm not afraid of bringing in the bikes after dark, either. I wonder what happened? This is rather mysterious.

Perhaps confidence just grows as we get older.

January 20

Trustworthiness has to be earned.

Last night I heard my mother say she didn't think she could trust my sister to go to the store by herself. I wonder why? Did she think Cindy would spend some of the money on candy rather than what was on Mother's list? I think I'll ask her what she meant. I wonder if she trusts me? Can you always be trusted?

Last year, my best friend told a secret I had shared with her. I was embarrassed because some of the kids in our class made fun of me. I told Mother about this and she said that maybe I shouldn't trust Penny anymore. Trust is important. I want to be trusted, and I want to be able to trust my friends. Don't you?

I will think carefully about who I can trust today. If there is someone I'm not sure of, I will choose another friend to share my thoughts with.

Disappointment is bound to happen on a daily basis.

Life is full of disappointments. Last week I really wanted to go to the movie with my older brother, but he didn't want to take me, and Mom said he didn't have to. He had already made plans with some of his friends. Dad didn't get the promotion at work that he had counted on. I heard him talking on the phone to his brother about it. He was super disappointed. I think he was mad, too. My grandmother said she wanted to win the lottery. Of course, we all want to win that. Almost everybody gets that disappointment every week.

Mom says we learn from our disappointments. She says disappointments are part of life and it's important to handle them gracefully. For instance, when my brother said no to the movie, I could have thrown a temper tantrum or I could have talked about my disappointment with a friend and then made other plans. It's pretty clear which would have been the graceful choice.

The next time I'm disappointed I will try to handle it with grace.

January 22

Surrender means giving in to another person or another opinion.

Last week in history class we read about a battle between a tribe of Native Americans and some settlers. Neither side wanted to surrender. It was a sad story because so many people died. I watch the news with my parents sometimes, and it's full of stories of people dying. Is it because no one ever wants to give in?

I don't like to give in when Brittany argues with me over whose turn it is to choose up sides for soccer. She always wants more than her share of turns. We don't get much playing done some days. Maybe it would be better to surrender my turn than to not play. What do you think? Do you have friends like Brittany?

Giving in might feel good. I will try it today.

Patience is a virtue worth learning.

Do your parents ever tell you to be patient? The first time my mother said that I was confused. I thought a patient was someone who was sick in the hospital. Of course, I was really young then. Having patience is different. I understand that now. It means being able to relax and wait for the outcome of a situation. I am not patient when I'm hungry and dinner isn't ready. My dad isn't patient when he wants me to clean up the mess I left at his computer table. And can he yell when I don't move fast!

Wanting something immediately is not being patient, is it? If adults can't always be patient, how can we kids be patient? Patience is something we learn, my grandmother says, and she seems patient most of the time. She seldom yells at anyone, except her cat when he scratches her furniture. Maybe I should ask her how she does it. Are you patient?

Learning to be patient will keep me from being bossy.

January 24

Apologizing when I've been inconsiderate is a good habit to form.

Saying you're sorry is seldom easy. Even when I know that I've done something mean, I don't like to admit it. Last week I hid my brother's jacket because I didn't want him to find it when it was time to go to the movie. I wanted Mom to get irritated with him. I don't even know why, except that his whining irritates me. She suspected I had hidden the jacket and got mad at me. I didn't get to go to the movie with the rest of the family, and I had to apologize to my brother.

I do know, though, that when someone apologizes to me, I really like it. An apology takes away some of my hurt or anger.

If I have hurt or irritated someone, I need to apologize.

Are only the young innocent?

Mother says my little sister, Anita, is innocent in how she thinks. She's too young to understand all the grown-up subjects we talk about at the dinner table. Monday night we talked about being grateful for all the blessings our family has received. Having Anita as a little sister is one of the blessings, even though she doesn't understand what we mean when we say it.

Innocence also means not being guilty when accused of committing a wrong act. I am quite relieved to be innocent in those situations. One happened recently at school. I don't even want to think about it anymore, but am I glad I was the innocent one.

Innocence can apply to each of us more than once a day. I will notice how it applies to me.

January 26

Our talents are our strengths.

No matter how hard I try I can't play soccer as well as Teresa. She is so strong. Dad says we all have our own talents. Mine just happens to be in math. I won the prize in the sixth grade for scoring the highest on the statewide tests. My parents were proud of me. Even my grandmother came to the award ceremony. The plaque is still hanging on my bedroom wall.

My mom is talented at the piano. She can play many songs by heart, which is good because she can never find her glasses. My friend Shelly gets lots of A's on her book reports. I guess you could say her talent lies in writing and thinking. I'm glad we all have something we're good at. For sure, we all have things we aren't so good at.

It's important to exercise my own talents and to appreciate and applaud the talents of others.

A friend can tell you things
you don't want to tell yourself.
Frances Ward Weller

I have been sad since Renee moved away. She has been my best friend since first grade. That was seven years ago. She lives in another state and I may never see her again. Yesterday we talked about how sad we are at school because many of us miss Renee. Mr. Talbot, my English teacher, says we will have this kind of sad experience many times in our lives. Change will occur whether we want it or not.

Having friends is important, but I'm worrying that another friend will move away. Mother says the best way to live is to have more than one really good friend, then I will always have someone to hang out with.

If I have two or three best friends, perhaps the world will be a warmer place.

January 28

There was a definite process by which one made people into friends, and it involved talking to them and listening to them for hours at a time.

Rebecca West

Our class went on a picnic last week with a seventh-grade class from another school. The teacher said it was an experiment in getting to know someone new. She and the other teacher are friends and had talked about the importance of making new friends. Boy, did I dread this experiment.

Guess what? It was fun. We started by playing a game. We each had to choose someone we didn't know. We each had to ask our partner as many questions as we could in five minutes to learn about each other. Then we had to introduce our new friend to the group. Stella, my new friend, likes to write science fiction, just like me. What a surprise!

Every friend I have was once a stranger to me.
I think I will make a new friend today.

In all the world, there is no one else like me.

Virginia Satir

Wishing I were more like someone else is something I do often. My mother tells me that a lot of people do that. She wishes she had hair as curly as her boss's. My dad wishes he just had more hair. He's getting bald already. Every time I see Holly at school, I envy her because she has more friends than anyone else in my class.

Mother says comparing myself with Holly or other girls is a waste of time. I am me! She keeps saying that I'm just right the way I am. She even says that other girls probably envy me about something. That's hard for me to imagine.

I am who I need to be. When I start to compare myself with someone, I can think of all the things I like about me.

January 30

True prayer is not asking God for love;
it is learning to love.

Mary Baker Eddy

I ate dinner at my friend's house last night. Cara's dad asked her to say grace and she said a neat prayer. I was impressed. I wondered if she knew it by heart or if she made it up on the spot. At my house we don't say prayers before we eat. I wonder why? Sometimes I pray when I go to bed. When I was a little girl Mom suggested that I do that. Now that I'm older, it helps me sleep better when I remember to say a prayer.

Do you pray before meals in your home? I think I'll talk to my parents about this. I noticed that everyone in Cara's family spoke politely to each other throughout the meal. I wonder if it was because they had prayed first? Sometimes my family argues when we're eating dinner.

Praying helps you feel more peaceful.

Nobody gets their way all the time.

I hit my little sister last night and now I can't go to Teri's for the sleepover, which doesn't seem fair. I fought with her because she drew on my book report before I turned it in. Mom agreed she shouldn't have done that, but said Nellie is only a baby and doesn't understand. I was supposed to take responsibility for the situation because I left the report on the couch. I always get blamed for Nellie's messes!

Do you ever feel sorry for yourself? Mom says we generally feel sorry for ourselves when we don't get our way, and that I'd better get used to not getting my way all the time because that's the way life works! Adults don't get their way all the time, either.

I will try to remember that not getting my way is OK. Something probably will happen today to help me remember this.

February

Inner thoughts determine outer behavior.

My sister keeps a diary. She writes in it every day after dinner. I would love to sneak a peek, but I can't find where she hides it. I know because I've looked for it! I asked what kinds of things she wrote about, and she said she was keeping track of all her activities and her thoughts. Mom said she kept a diary when she was young. Now she writes in a notebook that she calls a journal. She said it's pretty much the same thing as a diary. It's a way of checking up on how much she has changed over time.

I'm thinking about keeping a journal. I've changed a lot since I was little. Writing in a journal could be like writing to a best friend, one who is always there and ready to listen.

Writing down my thoughts could be helpful to me.

February 2

Wisdom not gained from within
is only someone else's knowledge.

Georgette Vickstrom

Last week every person in my class was assigned a word as the topic for an essay. My word was "wisdom." I decided to create a story, rather than an essay, that expressed its meaning. When we read them Friday, the class was impressed, and Mr. Browning was, too.

My story described how we learn and grow wise from the difficult things we go through. A main character in my story was my grandmother, who lost a brother when she was fifteen and whose house burned down when she was thirty. She's always reminding me that material things are temporary and that showing love to our loved ones is what's most important.

Wisdom is inner knowledge. If I am confused about what to do sometimes, I can knock on the door of my inner wisdom.

Never be afraid to sit awhile and think.

Lorraine Hansberry

Do you take a moment to be quiet before reacting when a person does something that upsets you? It's not easy to do, but Mrs. Liu, my Scout leader, told us a good story last week that explained this idea. The story was about Randi, a girl who lived next door to a grouchy old man. Randi and her friends were playing softball in her backyard and the ball rolled under the man's porch. When they went over to get it, he was waiting for them and he was mad. He kept the ball, too. They went back to Randi's yard and called him names.

The next day, Randi heard someone calling for help and discovered it was the old man. He had fallen in his yard. Randi thought about ignoring him, but she knew that wasn't the right thing to do. She went for help. The man gave the ball back to her and said he was sorry that he had kept it. This story really made me think.

I feel best when I am willing to be kind and forgiving.

February 4

Truth is the only safe ground to stand upon.

Elizabeth Cady Stanton

I peeked at my Christmas presents one year. Mother had hidden them, and when she was at work, I found them. I enjoyed peeking, but when Christmas morning came, I was sad because I had seen everything already. I felt sad for a long time for having been dishonest. I finally told my mom what I had done, and she seemed to understand. I learned a good lesson.

Being dishonest in any way can hurt you. Mother says that even if no one ever finds out you did something dishonest, you always know it and that memory can haunt you. I've learned that she's right. Have you had an experience like this?

Sometimes my mind tells me to do something that I know isn't honest. Being honest takes effort.

To fear is one thing.
To let fear grab you by the tail
and swing you around is another.

Katherine Paterson

Being afraid makes me self-conscious. I don't like for others to know when I'm afraid. When I was young I told my best friend that I was afraid of being called on to read aloud, and she told everybody in my class. They didn't laugh at me, but I could tell they thought I was stupid. I was embarrassed and afraid at the same time.

Mrs. LaSalle reminded the group that it was rude to share someone's secret. Then she told us about some of her fears. She was afraid of the dark until she was a teenager. Everyone has fear about something. I got over being afraid to read aloud right after we talked about it.

I have bigger fears now that I'm older, but I still try to tell someone about them. It makes them smaller right away.

February 6

To be selfish is to feel alone.

Have you ever had a particular treasure that you wanted to keep for yourself? And even when a best friend asked to borrow it for a while, you made an excuse for not sharing it? I'm that way with my CD collection. Lisa doesn't have any CDs and always wants to listen to mine. I'm not afraid she'll wreck them. I don't know why I don't want to share. I just don't. The problem is that I dread her asking the same question when I know I'm going to say no.

My older sister seems to enjoy sharing everything she has with her friend Erin. Maybe I could try to be more willing to share my CDs today and see how that makes me feel.

Sharing warms your heart.

Receiving compliments
inspires us to work even harder.

How does it make you feel when an adult compliments you? Last week I received a lot of compliments at school. Even the principal noticed how helpful I was in the cafeteria.

Mom says praise is a nice thing to offer others and receive from others. Considering how happy it makes me, I think I will see how it feels to make someone else happy by praising them. I've noticed that Rachel is really polite to the younger kids on the school bus every day. Maybe I could praise her for that. Can you think of someone you could praise today?

Doing something that makes another person feel good makes the doer feel good, too.

I am me and I am OK.

Virginia Satir

My mother is always looking in the mirror to see how she looks. Even when we walk by store windows, I notice that she tries to catch a glimpse of her reflection in the window. My dad kids her all the time, saying she looks great; after all, he wanted to marry her. But she thinks she's too fat. We don't get treats at our house often because Mom says she can't stay away from them if they're around.

I've been noticing how I look and I think my hair is too straight. I wish it were curly like Emily's. My legs are skinny, too. I almost always wear pants to cover them up. Everybody has parts of themselves that they don't like. Dad is always saying how lucky I am that my teeth are naturally straight and so white. He had to have braces when he was a kid.

Finding something about yourself that you like is important. I will make a list today of my likes.

How desperately we wish to maintain
our trust in those we love!

Sonia Johnson

Can your mother trust that you'll do what she's asked you to? Yesterday I said I would clean the fish tank and forgot to when I got home from gymnastics. Sometimes I just have too many things on my mind. Goldie, my favorite fish, doesn't care if the tank is dirty, but some things I forget can cause problems. When I was really little, I turned the water on in the bathroom sink to float a plastic fish and went outside. Water ended up in the hallway. And I ended up in my bedroom.

Being trustworthy is important. Mother says our friends and our families need to be able to count on us. Of course we need to be able to count on them, too. My sister can't always be counted on. She stays out all night once in a while and worries us. When one person in the family can't be counted on to do the right thing, it upsets everyone.

I want to be counted on to do what I said I would today.
There's only one way to make sure that happens.

February 10

Anxiety shadows every one of us sometime.

Do you ever feel nervous about something coming up? Do you ever feel sick to your stomach or do your hands ever shake when you think about something you have to do? My mother says this is a normal response for many people. She gets nervous and can't eat breakfast on the mornings that she has to give a speech at work.

She says it helps to share her fears with a friend. This helps her realize that she did her best to prepare and it's time to relax. Perhaps if I remember to talk about my fears when I'm anxious, I could relax, too. The big history test coming up on Friday would be a good time to practice this.

Anxiety is normal, but so is talking about our fears. I will put this idea into practice soon.

In the face of an obstacle that is impossible to overcome, stubbornness is stupid.
Simone de Beauvoir

Dad hates to help Mom with the laundry. He says he likes washing the dishes and doesn't mind going grocery shopping, but he can't fold clothes to suit Mom. Whenever she asks for help with the laundry, he finds an excuse to get out of it. I'm this way, too, about some of my chores. Are you? Whenever it's time to clean my closet or hang up a whole pile of clothes, I suddenly feel tired. Mom says I'm stubborn.

I suppose if everybody found a reason to skip some of their chores, we would live in a pretty messy world. Just think what it would be like if everybody in a family was stubborn all at the same time. What a mess! No clean dishes. No clean clothes. I guess doing my part is important.

I will carry out my responsibilities today.
My family needs to be able to count on me.

February 12

As a human being, you have no choice about the fact that you need a philosophy.

Ayn Rand

My grandmother says that being thankful for all the wonderful parts of her life keeps her from feeling sad about the parts that aren't good. For instance, her house needs to be painted, but she's thankful she has a roof over her head, a working refrigerator, and hot running water. Not everybody has a place to live. In my city, a lot of men, women, and children are homeless.

Mother thinks Grandma has a good philosophy, which means knowing what to say and how to feel about the situations that come up every day. It's like having something already in your mind that you use to measure how you feel about particular circumstances. Deciding to be thankful for the good parts and putting the not-so-good ones out of your mind is a good philosophy to have, I think.

I will try to be more like an older person I respect.

Blaming is often the easy way out.

My sister blames me for so many things. Yesterday she couldn't find her favorite sweater when it was time for the bus. She told Mom she was sure I had put it some place. I hadn't even seen her sweater! Most people like to blame others when something goes wrong in their lives. When Mom backed into the station wagon next door last week, at first she claimed my dad had moved the rearview mirror! Being responsible for everything that happens to us is a big job.

Just this morning I spilled my milk when I was pouring it over my cereal. Right away I began to blame my younger sister, saying she bumped the table when I was pouring the milk. She hadn't really bumped the table. I just didn't want to get blamed for making a mess. Do you rush to blame others, too?

Learning to accept responsibility is part of growing up.
I won't blame another person for anything I do today.

February 14

Do not compare yourself with others.

Barbara Kimball

Tanya got another new bike. She has had three new bikes since I met her. My dad repairs my sister's old bikes for me as she outgrows them. It doesn't seem fair, but Dad says our family can't afford all the things Tanya's family can. We have four kids in our family and she's an only child. Sometimes I wish I didn't have any sisters or brothers.

In Scouts the other day, we talked about envy. Our leader said that we shouldn't be ashamed of our envy. It's common to all of us; however, it's better to be happy for others rather than envious of them. Probably Tanya is lonely sometimes because she doesn't have a sister to play cards with on rainy days. Maybe she is even envious of me occasionally!

I will try to be happy today, for me and for my friends.

Face the thing you fear,
and you do away with that fear.

Anonymous

Once in a while I'm afraid I can't succeed in anything. Do you ever have that fear? Whether I'm studying for a math test or a science quiz (and science is my best subject) or practicing my piano for a recital, I'm scared that I'll mess up and look foolish. I feel better if I talk over my fear with someone else, but often I'm too embarrassed. The problem is that if I don't tell Mom or Dad, or maybe my older sister, I don't get the pep talk I need. Mom says everybody, not just me, needs encouragement.

It's interesting how having someone I trust tell me that I will do OK takes away most of my fear. Mom says having someone else share your fear is what really helps. The thing is, you have to tell someone else about your fear if you want them to share it.

If I'm afraid about something today, I will courageously share my feelings with someone who cares about me.

February 16

They buried the hatchet,
but in a shallow, well-marked grave.
Dorothy Walworth

Wanting my own way often ends up in an argument. My friend usually wants her way, too. My history teacher says conflicts between countries happen in the same way. Wars get fought because the leaders of the opposing countries want their own way. It seems that not much good ever comes out of quarreling. When my friend and I don't agree, we go home mad.

Perhaps my friend and I could agree to disagree. It might be a fun experiment. Maybe we could take turns being right or getting our own way. One day I could agree to go along with her plan and the next day she could go along with my plan. Compromising makes more sense than not having someone to hang out with because of an argument.

Today is a good day to ask someone to experiment with taking turns being right or getting our own way.

Worrying so clouds our mind
that we can't hear God's messages.
Susan Ebaugh

My aunt Karen says I worry too much. I worry about being called on in class and not knowing the answer. I worry whether my friends will invite me to their parties. I worry that the bus will come early and I'll miss it. Most kids would be glad if that happened.

Aunt Karen says there's a way to not worry so much. She writes down her worries in a list or a letter to herself. She talks to a friend about what she writes down. This helps her take positive actions. If I talk about my worries with someone I trust, then maybe my worry load will be lighter.

I may need to write a few letters today, depending on how worried I feel.

February 18

Anger is a wind
which blows out the lamp of the mind.

Source unknown

Is there one thing that makes you angrier than anything else? My dad seems to get angriest at his boss. My mom gets angry when my brother and I fight over whose turn it is to work at the computer. She said yesterday that she wished my dad had never bought it. I get angry when I study hard for a test and get a lower grade than Beth. I get mad about lots of things at school.

I read a story last week during library period about an angel who helped an angry girl figure out what she needed to do with her anger and then swept away her angry thoughts. All she had to do was make a picture of the angel in her mind and the angel came to her. I wonder if an angel like that could help me with my angry times?

Today might be a good day to start picturing an angel in my mind.

To love deeply in one direction
makes us more loving in all others.

Anne-Sophie Swetchine

Showing your love can happen in many ways. You don't really have to say "I love you." Showing it in your actions might be even more important than saying the words. Miss Jackson asked us to write down a list of the ways our parents showed us they loved us. My list was really long. I noticed that Hayley didn't make one. My dad once explained to me that Hayley's parents were alcoholics. She must feel lonely and confused.

Then the teacher suggested we make a list throughout the week of the ways we had shown others that we loved them. That list wasn't nearly as long. This exercise made me think about some of the ways I could start showing my love. I've been thinking about trying to show Hayley that I care about her.

I will see how many new ways I can show my love today.

February 20

Liking ourselves isn't always easy.

Lots of times I don't feel good about the way I'm acting. In the past three days, I have gossiped about my best friend, Lanie, taken some change out of my sister's purse, and lied to my parents about where I went after school. Last week, even though I didn't do it, I thought about skipping school with Andrea. It's not easy to like myself when all these things are on my mind.

My mom told me about "exercises" I can do to help me like myself better. I can be kind to everyone in my family. I can speak politely to every adult or child who crosses my path. I can apologize to Lanie for gossiping about her, and I can choose to be friends with girls who don't skip school. Doing what I know is the right thing makes it easier to like myself.

It's easier to like myself when my actions match what I know to be the right thing.

A miracle is a state of mind.

Kathryn Ebaugh

What are miracles? Our minister said that when Jesus healed the sick, he was performing miracles. My grandmother is hoping for a miracle every time she buys a lottery ticket. I rode my new bike across Turner Street, the busiest street in our neighborhood, and I knew it was a miracle that the dirty red truck that pulled out in front of me didn't hit me.

In a book Mother bought at the church bookstore, it says that miracles are the result of changing our minds about something. The girl in the first story in the book hated the new kids in her neighborhood. They ran through her yard and never asked her to join them. One day she asked God to help her feel better. The youngest girl in the new family came over one day and said she would like to be friends. They laughed and had fun for the rest of the summer. That was a miracle. It was a good story, too.

If all I have to do is change my mind in a positive way about something today, it should be easy to have at least one miracle.

February 22

Trying to control another person
is like trying to make water run uphill.
Thelma Kirkpatrick

I can't make a single one of my friends do what I want them to do unless they really want to do it. That's hard to understand. Brad, Jennifer, and I were ready to play softball yesterday, but Holly said no. She wanted to read a book about the presidents' wives. We needed her so we could have an even number on each side. Do you think we could talk her into it? No way!

Mom says we all want to control others. She even has trouble making my sister and me do what she wants us to do. She can take away a treat we had counted on or a plan to go to the movie if we don't do what she wants. I guess I'll have to change my plan if I can't change someone else's plan.

All I can count on controlling is myself.

We must all lean upon others.

Margaret Collier Graham

I'm not always eager to help when Mom or Dad ask me to. Often when they need help, I'm in the middle of a good game on the computer and I don't want to stop. Yesterday I kept playing when Dad asked me to clean the garage. The consequences were not good. I have to stay off the computer for three days. I won't get my book report handed in on time. Dad wasn't even fazed when I told him that.

I know that helping others is important, even though I'm slow to do it. My homeroom teacher often mentions the value of helping others. Last week she asked for volunteers to help the fifth-graders who were having trouble reading. I raised my hand because I enjoy tutoring younger kids.

I can be helpful to someone today. Opportunities to be helpful will come at home and school.

February 24

Choosing an occupation
doesn't have to be accidental.

My dad is a firefighter, and he loves it. There are women firefighters at my dad's station, too. That's what I might choose to be someday. Driving a huge truck would be neat, I think.

My mom was a nurse before she got sick. She helped to deliver babies. I used to think I wanted to do that. She said I should study to be a doctor or a nurse. She can't live with us anymore because of how serious her illness is. Dad says he's glad he loves his job because it helps him not miss my mom so much.

We never know how our lives will change. If I love my job when I grow up, it will help me get through tough times in my life.

I will take the time to look into occupations. I'm glad I have lots of time to find a career I will love.

Asking for help is no easy task.

Everyone needs help with something once in a while. My dad takes his car to a garage because he can't repair it himself. He and Mom hire a woman to help clean our house. Mr. Bradley has to get help from Mrs. Novak, the principal, when the seventh-grade boys fight in the lunchroom.

Last week I needed help with my homework nearly every night. Was I ever lucky that my brother Tommy was home. He helped me with the entire science assignment. Science isn't my best subject. I almost never need help with math or history. Tommy is not good at penmanship. Maybe I can help him so people can read what he writes.

I won't be shy if I need help at school or home.
If I can offer to help someone else today, I will.

February 26

Praise is acknowledgment
that everyone deserves.

Dad came home from work excited last night because his boss had congratulated him in front of his whole department for a report he wrote. He was proud to get all that praise in front of his co-workers. Praise for something we do, for a small job like cleaning the basement or for something big like getting chosen to be class president, makes us feel good. Why is praise so important?

Mom said it's because when we receive praise, it's a sign that we've been noticed. Have you ever felt invisible? I used to when I was small. Lots of times no one talked to me. I wondered if they couldn't see me. I knew this was a silly thought, but I had it anyway. Praise lets us know that we are seen and appreciated.

I like praise. I like to be noticed.

Strangers can't always be trusted.

I wish I didn't have to be so careful about strangers. My mother said that when she was a girl, she never had to worry about walking someplace alone, even when it was dark. Now adults warn us almost every day about the danger around us. Either my mom or a friend's mom takes us everyplace we have to go. I feel like a baby getting taken and picked up all the time, but I know it's because adults worry, and for a good reason.

I wonder what makes a person harm someone he or she doesn't even know? Mother says it's usually because they are unhappy adults. Perhaps they didn't have a happy childhood. I sure can't imagine that I would ever want to harm an innocent child. There are many good people in the world, but I need to be leery of strangers.

Although it makes me sad, I need to be cautious and protect myself around strangers.

The choice to express love or to express sarcasm occurs in the slightest moment.

How we talk to one another is important. Yesterday my grandmother told me to quit being sarcastic to my little brother. I wasn't sure what she meant. I figured out that "sarcastic" meant making fun of somebody in a mean way that's sometimes disguised as humor. I think I'm sarcastic quite often.

When I'm being mean I don't like myself much, and the person I'm treating in a sarcastic way doesn't feel good, either. My stepmom says life is hard enough without us making it harder for each other by being mean. I know she's right.

I will have many chances today to be kind rather than sarcastic. I will open and stretch my heart in the direction of kindness.

All things can be borne.

Elizabeth Chase Akers

Last week I was counting on going fishing with my dad, and he forgot. I was sad because he often forgets about a plan we've made. Mom says one thing we have to learn as we grow up is that things don't always work out like we planned. Sometimes the people we love disappoint us. She felt bad for me, too.

She asked me what would help me feel better. I said inviting some friends over for a sleepover and making her delicious fudge. She laughed and said, "Great idea!"

When I am sad or disappointed, I can do something fun that takes my mind off my disappointment.

March

Showing affection can make two people happy.

I love it when my grandmother shows affection for me. I especially like it when she offers to give me a hug when she notices that I'm quiet. I usually get quiet when I'm worried about something. Her affection gives me strength, and I need it pretty often ever since my dad moved out of our house.

She says that everyone needs affection. This seems hard to believe. My older brother acts tough. Grandmother says that acting tough often covers up a big need for affection. I've noticed that he doesn't push her away when she gives him a hug. Grandmother suggested that I notice all the ways people express a need for affection, and then try to offer them some. Right away I realized that my friend Simone needs affection by the way she clings to anyone close to her.

Showing affection will change how I look at my experiences today.

March 2

The way I treat others most likely will be the way they treat me.

Mom says that how we treat others comes back to us. It works like this: If I am nasty to Mom or my brother, neither of them will feel like being nice to me. The opposite can be true, too. For instance, when we go out of our way to be kind, especially to someone who is not expecting it, that person usually will be kind back to us. Can you think of a time when this worked for you?

Mom says that this idea doesn't work immediately with some people. For example, she baked cookies for the neighbor who had been mad at her because our dog ran through her flowers. Mrs. Donnelly didn't even say thank you. But a week or so later, she brought over some homemade jam and said she was sorry she had not been friendlier.

The way I treat someone today will come back to me.

How we handle our anger
tells others a lot about who we are.

Some days I seem to be mad at everyone, and I don't know why. Usually when I'm feeling that way I want to blame it on my mom or my little sister, Lilly, or even my poor dog. Sometimes Lilly has messed up my bedroom by pulling the covers off the bed or my T-shirts out of a dresser drawer, and sometimes the dog has chewed up a magazine I was saving. But some days, nobody has done anything in particular and I'm mad anyway.

One sign that you're growing up is being able to feel anger without taking it out on others or blaming them for what is making you mad. No matter what has happened, we don't have to let our anger control us. I wouldn't like it if Lilly tore up a picture I had painted. But I could choose to understand that she's young and doesn't realize when she's done something wrong. Can you look at what happens with less anger?

If I get angry today, I can acknowledge my feelings,
but I don't have to let my anger control me.

March 4

The opinion we have of ourselves isn't just based on beliefs; it's also based on actions.

Marie Lindquist

Last week Mr. Riley had our class do an interesting exercise. He called it a personal inventory. We had to make two lists of words that described how we generally acted toward other people. We put favorable words on one list and less favorable words on the other list. Then he paired us with another student and we shared our lists. He said this exercise was to help us realize who we really were.

I was paired with Rebecca. We had the word "bossy" on our lists. We had "shy," too. I realized that many of us are alike. I learned a lot about myself.

What I learn about myself shows me what I may need to work on changing.

We're growing out of the old and into the new.
Jan Lloyd

Most of the girls in my class are nice, but my parents think a few are too worldly for me. For instance, Megan wears heavy makeup to school and started dating older boys when she was in middle school. Actually, I wouldn't even want to look like her. Jennifer is another girl who's not a great example. My older sister knows her older sister and said Jennifer smokes after school and has done drugs.

My mom says our choice of friends is important. I can be kind to everyone, but if I hang out with people who do their homework and don't smoke and are involved in activities, that will help me be a strong and positive person.

I want to make healthy choices in my actions and friendships.

March 6

In childhood I was told that if I have faith, health, and love, I have everything. As an adult I know it's true.

Mardy Kopischke

Do you know what it means to have faith? It means having the feeling that everything is going to be OK regardless of how a situation looks. My grandfather was the first to talk to me about faith. He said it gave him strength every day. When my parents got divorced, I was sure that I would never see my dad again. My grandfather suggested that having faith could help me feel better. It did.

Mom says appreciating our health and feeling love are as important as having faith. The best way to appreciate our health is to treat our bodies well. Eat right, get a lot of sleep, and exercise, too. But feeling love is the best of all. It changes how everything in our life looks. Try it and you'll see what I mean.

I'm glad that I have faith, appreciate my health, and am willing to let others know that I love them.

Making the best of a situation is good enough.

"When life gives you lemons, make lemonade." This means make the best of a bad situation. For example, our whole family was going to work in the yard Saturday. Dad was in charge of raking and bagging leaves. Mom was in charge of cleaning the porch. My brother and I were the "gophers" for them. In the middle of the jobs, it began to rain hard. Mom was disappointed because we had all agreed to help. She made the most of the situation, though. She assigned us jobs in the house.

The closets got straightened out and so did the basement. She said maybe it was good that it rained. Working inside isn't as much fun as being outside, but we had no choice. She has already asked us to do the outside work next week. The best part of all was that she made brownies as a special treat after the work was done.

Disappointments happen. I will try to make something good out of the next one.

March 8

Being grateful isn't always what I feel like being!

Sandra Elliott

Every time I begin to moan and complain, my dad says, "Count your blessings." I hate to be reminded, particularly when I'm in a mood to complain, but I have noticed that when I do look at the great things in my life, like my new bike and how much I love riding it, my crummy attitude begins to change. I still fight the attitude change occasionally, especially when Mom makes me do chores before I can play with my friends or talk on the phone.

Just for fun, see how many blessings you can come up with in sixty seconds. Ask a friend to watch the clock. My list includes my bed and my comforter. I'm thankful that I have some new clothes, not all hand-me-downs. Today I'm really thankful that my dad is coming back from a trip. I haven't seen him for ten days.

I will start my day today by remembering some of my blessings.

Satisfaction comes from hard work and acceptance, not from being hard on ourselves.

How satisfied are you with yourself? For instance, if you studied hard for your history exam but got only fifteen of the twenty questions right, you might not be satisfied with yourself. You might realize you need to study even harder. Another test of your satisfaction might be your appearance. Are you constantly comparing yourself with other girls and judging yourself harshly? It's hard to stay satisfied. My grandfather says human beings are too quick to condemn themselves. He says we should be more like the creatures in the animal world.

Sometimes I am satisfied. My painting turned out great in art class. My dad got it framed and hung it in his office. Being satisfied with myself is a lot more fun than not being happy with how I'm doing. What it takes for me to be satisfied is hard work and then acceptance of how things turn out. I sometimes forget that part of the equation.

If I want to feel satisfied today, I have to do my part.

March 10

Pain and chaos give me a chance for transformation.
Carlotta Posz

Transformation means to change. For sure, all of us have changed a lot since we were in kindergarten. We've grown taller, we're much smarter, and we're no doubt afraid of fewer things than when we were five or six years old. These kinds of changes have come with simply getting older.

Change can happen as a result of painful experiences, too. For instance, when my grandfather died, Grandma moved in with us. She was sad for a long time, and it meant that my brother and I had to be gentle with her. We learned how to be more considerate. Her pain helped transform us. Mom is happy about this.

Another example of pain creating transformation was when Sophie decided to drop me as her best friend. I was heartbroken. Mom said the only solution was to seek another best friend. Had this not happened, I would not be going on vacation with Holly and her family this summer. Transformation can be good, wouldn't you say?

I will look on change as an opportunity for something better in my life.

Negotiating differences is a sign of growing up.

Yesterday my mom was furious with me. She repeatedly said, "Why don't you just do what I say?" I can't explain it. I just seem to have my own ideas about certain things. For instance, she hates the fingernail polish that's "in." She said it makes me look tough. We fight, too, about the clothes I buy with my baby-sitting money. My best friend and I buy a lot of identical shirts.

She says she doesn't want to control me, but she does want me to consider her ideas. I know she's smart. She has an important job with a big company, so I know they must think a lot of her ideas are good. Perhaps I need to listen more. It's no fun to be in a war with her every night, that's for sure. Dad says people are sometimes too independent. I wonder if that's what he thinks I am.

If I disagree with someone today, I will suggest we try to negotiate our differences.

March 12

One life stamps and influences another.

Mary Kay Blakely

Being influenced means letting the behavior of others affect you. Last year, for instance, I spent part of every day with Kristen. She was generally bossy to the younger kids. Without even thinking about it, I started to get bossy, too. I hadn't even realized this until my mom pointed it out. She also reminded me that Kristen didn't have many friends. She thought maybe that was why.

I am not sure if that was why Kristen had so few friends, but I felt a lot happier when I started to spend more time with Tanya. She also included others in her activities and made everyone feel welcome. Her friendliness made me friendlier, too. She was a good influence in my life. Do you have a good influence in your life?

I will try to be a good influence in someone else's life today. I will choose people who are a good influence for me.

Guilt is an emotion that has periodically served me well.

Barbara E. Marz

Sometimes I feel guilty because I blame something I did on my brother or sister and Mom believes me. My youngest sister can't tell on me because she can't talk yet, and Mom seldom believes my brother because he has a bad track record for lying. But because of the guilt I feel, it might be better if I just tell the truth. Do you ever try to get away with something and feel lousy about it?

Dad says that guilt weighs us down. It takes away our energy and enthusiasm. Nothing is much fun if your mind is overcome by guilt. Just last week I lied about who knocked the vase off the piano. Mom cleaned it up and didn't say anything. But then when I went to Tracy's house for dinner, I didn't feel hungry. Her mother had made fried chicken, too, my favorite meal. I'm sure my guilt kept me from being hungry.

If I make a poor choice, I will listen to my guilt. It often tells me what I need to do to make things right.

March 14

Hope is the feeling you have
that the feeling you have isn't permanent.

Jean Kerr

Robbie's grandmother says having hope can change every aspect of your life. She told us a story about a family with a sick little girl. The dad lost his job and they had no insurance to pay the doctor's bill. They prayed together every day that the dad would get another job. They never gave up hope that a good job would come along. Finally one did. The new job offered him even better insurance than the old one had. Losing the first job turned out to be good luck in the end because now all the bills were paid. The little girl would not have lived without the medicine she could get with the new insurance.

The best thing about having hope is that it keeps you feeling better while you're going through a difficult time. My dad says that having hope is like keeping the door open for a new opportunity. If your door is always closed, nothing good can come in. Is your door open?

I will keep the door to my heart open by hoping for good things.

When people make changes in their lives, they may start by changing the way they talk about that subject.

Jean Illsley Clarke

If I'm feeling sad about something that was done or said to me, it's a good idea to talk this over with someone. Pretending that I don't have a certain feeling isn't helpful, ever. Like yesterday, Bridget said some unkind things about me to Heather, the new girl in our class. I was really upset. But as soon as I talked it over with my older sister, I was able to change my mood.

My grandmother taught me an interesting exercise. She said that when you're mad or sad or even just bored, you can "act as if" you are happy instead. It's best to share how you're feeling with another person first, though. But when you get good at "acting as if," you can become whatever you want to be every day. Not having to stay sad or mad is exciting, particularly when you probably thought, like I did, that you were stuck with whatever feeling was in your mind, maybe forever.

I can choose to feel happy from the minute I get up today. If I am feeling sad, it's time to share this with another person.

March 16

The past is gone forever.

Do you have trouble paying attention to what you are doing right now because you're thinking about something that happened earlier? Yesterday I missed the whole explanation of the new way to solve long division problems because I was thinking about the fight my dad and I had at the dinner table the night before. I was embarrassed to ask for another explanation. Thank goodness Mr. Whitney was nice about explaining it again. Actually, many of the kids needed another explanation.

Mother says we all have to learn to let go of the past. No matter what happened, we can't change it now. She says that we can learn from our mistakes. For instance, the fight with my dad was because I hadn't carried out the trash in time for the pickup. Now our trash has to sit in the garage until next week. I can remember to take out the trash next week, but I may as well quit thinking about the fight. It's over.

I can't change the past. I can make sure I don't repeat a mistake, though.

God's will never takes me
where his grace will not sustain me.

Ruth Humlecker

I've made a great discovery. When I'm afraid, I visualize God's warm arms holding me and my fear goes away. I didn't discover this by myself. My sister learned this in her church youth group. She said it worked for her. It worked for me the first time I tried it. I wonder why more people don't try this. Perhaps people simply don't talk about it. Not everybody is comfortable talking about spiritual things.

The first time I tried to visualize God was when I stayed overnight at my aunt Laura's house. I had never stayed there without my sister, and Laura has a big, dark house. When I went upstairs to bed, I was sure I could see ghosts hanging out in the bedroom. When she came up to check on me, I told her about the shadows, and she said it was just my imagination. I began to imagine God's arms instead and the shadows went away. I fell asleep fast.

Replacing my fear with an image of God is pretty simple.

March 18

Secrets can keep us stuck in the past.

Secrets can be fun sometimes, like when you and your best friend talk about your boyfriends, and you don't want anyone else to know what you have said. Keeping a secret about the birthday present you and your mom bought for your dad is OK, too. But sometimes you may have a secret that doesn't feel so good.

They told us at school, in the first grade I think, that we should not keep it secret if someone has touched us in a private place or said things to us that were not nice. Certain things should not be secrets, ever. I was glad they told us that because not long after, a friend of mine had an uncle who tried to touch her in a private place. I told her to tell her mom. I hope I can always tell the difference between the fun secrets and the other kind. Can you?

If I have any doubt about a certain secret today, perhaps I should tell it to my Mom, Dad, or a teacher I trust.

It is a peaceful thing to be one succeeding.

Gertrude Stein

Do you ever wonder if you will be really good at anything when you grow up? I think about this a lot. Mom says I worry too much. She says that everybody has a particular talent that guarantees success. I sure wonder what mine will be. So far I'm not very good in algebra, and I'm pretty bad in science. Actually, I wish I were better at basketball. I would love to play for the WNBA someday. I'm good in English, though, and the teacher read a story I wrote to the class last week. Perhaps I'll be a writer after college.

I felt good when Ms. Sidney read my story. She said it was a real achievement to keep the class interested in a six-page story. I guess we do all have talent at something, and the more we use it the stronger it becomes.

Feeling successful is a wonderful feeling.

March 20

Choices are not irrevocable. . . . They can be remade.

Julie Reibe

Picking friends who are responsible and respectful, which clothes to wear to school, and what book to read next from the library are choices I get to make. I can ask for help with my choices, but I have to make them. When I was younger, Mom and Dad made most choices for me. Even though it's more interesting to be making my own choices, it's difficult sometimes.

I worry over some of my choices. For instance, when Mom says I can have only one friend sleep over, I worry that I'll insult the friend I had to leave out. Last year I invited Shawn, a new girl in our class, to spend the night. Was I surprised to discover that she smoked cigarettes. I had to ask her to put them away. I never felt comfortable around her after that. There is a lot to think about when it comes to our choices.

Making choices is one of the responsibilities of growing up. It is exciting and difficult.

Saying "yes" means I really do want
to change my life for the better.

Liane Cordes

Being a complainer is no fun. Being friends with someone who complains all the time isn't fun, either. I used to spend time with Amy after school, but she became such a complainer that I seldom go over to her house unless I'm lonely and have no one else to talk with. Have you ever felt this way about someone?

Mom says some people see the glass as half empty rather than half full. Those who complain all the time are seeing the glass as half empty. She calls this negative thinking. My grandfather thinks negative a lot. He complains about my grandmother's cooking and housecleaning and about "kids these days." I wonder how this kind of thinking begins? For surc, I don't want to become like him or Amy.

I want to be a positive person today.

March 22

Your conscience keeps you on your toes.

"Let your conscience be your guide" is a saying my mother uses a lot. She reminded me of this yesterday. I tripped my sister when she was running down the hall, and then I ducked into my bedroom so Mom couldn't see me. But worse than that, I pretended I hadn't even been out of my room. My sister fell on her sore leg and screamed in pain. I was ashamed but I was even more embarrassed to admit my part in her fall.

I know I'm old enough to know the difference between right and wrong. When I do the wrong thing, even if it seems that I'm getting away with it, I know in my heart that I'm wrong. My conscience doesn't let me forget it. Actually, I believe it's good that our conscience is always checking up on us, because we might be tempted to avoid taking responsibility when we're wrong.

I will try to keep my conscience happy today.

Many of us have a mean streak.
The important thing is to shrink it, not exercise it.

Do you ever feel compelled to do something mean? Sometimes an idea comes into my mind to do something that my heart tells me is wrong. Last week I was walking down the street and noticed that our grouchy neighbor hadn't picked up his morning paper yet. I could have put it by his front door, but I kicked it under the bushes before I even considered what I was doing. By then it was too late. I couldn't even reach the paper. I'm sure Mr. Thomas couldn't either.

Taking any action without thinking through the consequences is not smart. In a flash, I had made life harder for my neighbor, and I felt ashamed. My mom believes that if a person asks her heart if what she is about to do is the right thing, she will always know right from wrong.

Today I will stop before taking action and see if my heart agrees with me.

March 24

Help is often only a request away.

Many times a day you may have a problem you need help with. Sometimes I need help French-braiding my hair. Just last week I was writing an essay about female pilots and needed help to spell the word "aviation." I like having spell-check on the computer. Yesterday I needed help changing the sheets on my bed. Last time I managed by myself but this time I couldn't tuck the fitted sheet under the mattress. Dad was close by and gave me a hand.

I hear Mom asking Dad to help her move the couch because she wants to vacuum the carpet. Dad even needs help from our neighbor sometimes. Last week Dad and our neighbor repaired the fence between our houses. If no one ever asked for help, many things would never get done.

Asking for help is nothing to be ashamed of.

Outcomes seldom match our expectations.

Lydia Ellis

Lots of things don't turn out like we hoped they would. I was sure my father would be able to attend my school banquet, but he got the flu. I was getting an award for an essay I wrote on democracy. I didn't want to go alone and Mom was attending a convention out of the city. Dad suggested I ask my neighbor who has no kids. Mr. Greenman was delighted I asked him. He even won a door prize.

We can't be sure things will turn out like we want them to. The important thing to remember is that things have a way of turning out for the best, no matter what has happened. It didn't seem good that Dad got sick, but maybe having Mr. Greenman come was good for him, and if Dad had been well, it wouldn't have happened that way. I will try to remember this when other situations disappoint me.

Whatever happens today will be for the best. Even if I'm not happy at first, there will be a "silver lining."

March 26

Sometimes we create a big stir over small problems.

Making a big deal out of an ordinary problem is easy to do. Mom says it's one of my main faults. For example, I couldn't find the shoelaces my dad had just bought for my new tennis shoes. I threw everything out of my dresser drawers in my search. I decided I couldn't go to school if I had to wear my old, dirty shoes. My parents and I had a big fight about that. I had to clean up the bedroom, too, before going to school, which meant I was late.

Mom says I make mountains out of molehills. I guess I do sometimes. When I came home from school that day, I found the laces under my bed. I wore them the next day to school, and waiting a day wasn't such a big deal.

I will try not to exaggerate anything today. It makes my life more complicated.

Habits are easily formed and hard to break.

A habit is doing something again and again, often without being aware of it. My mom has the habit of rubbing her right eye when she is talking. She doesn't even realize she is doing it. It's a bad habit for her to have because she wears contacts. I have the habit of coughing before I answer a question. I wasn't aware I did this until my math teacher mentioned it. Now I try to stop myself but it's hard to do.

Of course, there are good habits, too. For instance, I generally remember to say please and thank you. Adults love that habit. My dad remembers to say grace before dinner. My grandmother says that is one of the best habits a person can have. As we focus on making and keeping good habits, we are more able to let the bad ones go.

I will consider beginning a new, good habit today.

March 28

Practice can get a person close to being perfect.

Anything that you learn to do well takes practice. Dad makes hitting the softball look easy, but he has been playing on a team for many years. My mother can play the piano well. She took lessons for ten years when she was young. I wonder how many hours of practice that adds up to. So far, in my life, I haven't practiced hard at anything, but I'd better start practicing my list of state capitals if I hope to pass the test at the end of the year. There is room for practice in many areas.

I wish I didn't have to practice anything to be good at it. Of course, that's what everyone wishes. It doesn't work that way, though. Even doing a simple thing like making a bed takes practice to get all of the rumples smoothed out. Every single person who ever lived had to practice something. Do you know who Tiger Woods is? He is a famous golfer. He has been practicing golf since he was three years old.

I can begin practicing lots of things today. My schoolwork, a musical instrument, or a sport is a good place to start.

What we call failure is not the falling down,
but the staying down.

Mary Pickford

I got a D- on my last report card. I was nervous about showing it to my parents. My mom was upset. My dad was angry with me. I was ashamed. The reason for the D- was because I failed to turn in the homework on time. It was in a subject I understand, but I just never finished the assignments. The teacher said she hoped the D- taught me a lesson.

Learning by our mistakes is important. Since that report card, I haven't failed to turn in a single assignment. I have not received all A's, but I haven't been below a C on a single assignment. Another thing I've been prompt with is getting my chores at home done on time. Mom says the D- taught me a lot.

I will make sure I'm doing whatever work
is expected of me today.

March 30

Setting an example is everyone's assignment.

My little brother watches what I do. It's important for me to set a good example. We all learn by watching others. I learned much of what I know the same way. After watching the older girls playing soccer, I became pretty good. I watched a long time before I asked to join them, though.

Setting an example is done in many ways. Mother sets an example for our family by saying a prayer before dinner. Now whenever she has to work over the dinner hour, one of us says a prayer. Timothy, my older brother, gets into trouble for being rude when he answers the phone, which sets a bad example for us. Dad was the one calling yesterday when Timothy answered. I bet he'll be more careful now.

I can set a good example for anyone watching me today.

We do not always like what is good for us.
Eleanor Roosevelt

My Sunday school teacher says that everything happens for a reason. We may not understand it at the time, but in a few days or weeks, it will begin to make sense. This is hard for me to accept. My dog got run over last summer. I still don't understand that. My dad says what happened to the dog shows us how quickly a car can show up out of nowhere. Anyone of us could get run over if we aren't careful before crossing a street. Could that be the lesson in my dog's death?

If everything has a reason, perhaps trying to figure out the lesson for whatever happens is a good exercise. Sam got his bike stolen from the grocery store after school. The lesson there was to remember to lock up your bike, even if you are going to be inside for only a minute. All of us who are his friends learned that lesson with him.

I wonder what will happen today? It will be interesting to try to figure out the lesson in whatever happens.

April

Anger and worry are the enemies of clear thought.
Madeleine Brent

Our thoughts take charge of our actions. For instance, if you're angry with one of your siblings about whose job it is to clear the dinner table, you might slam the dishes so hard on the counter that you break one. This happened to me recently. Another thing that can happen is not hearing an important instruction in class because of worrying over something that happened earlier in the day. I missed an assignment last week because of this.

Keeping my mind free of "noise" (that's what my mom calls it) is a habit I'm trying to develop. Mom learned this habit when she studied meditation many years ago. She said no one is too young to practice clearing her mind. She told me that whatever is in my mind got there because I put it there, and I can replace any thought that isn't doing me much good. It's easier said than done, however.

I wonder what thoughts I will hold in my mind today?

April 2

Guidance in the form of a suggestion is most common.

At school we get guidance from the teacher. At home, our parents offer guidance. If we have older siblings, they give it, too. Guidance is a matter of sharing with others something good you have learned from your own experience. Have you received any guidance lately? Maybe your parents suggested that you stay away from the kids who are doing drugs. Mine sure did. Mine said I should stay away from the kids who get detention, too. And last week I was invited to a party where I knew there would be alcohol. I didn't even bother to ask if I could go.

Is there some guidance you might offer a friend today? I mentioned to Steph yesterday that she was snubbing the new girl in our class. I guess that was an example of guidance.

Guidance, when heard and followed, is one important way of learning how to behave.

Sadness is not an uncommon feeling.

Before my parents got divorced, I was seldom sad. At least, I don't remember being sad. Now there isn't much to laugh about. Almost every day I wish that Dad would move back home. Mom says it's not likely to happen, but she did promise that he would never quit loving Stacy and me.

Mom says that being sad can become a habit, and although she is often sad that my dad left, she is trying to master taking more control over her feelings every day. The way she does it is to remind herself that she doesn't have to dwell on the thoughts that make her sad. She says, "Don't go there, Carol," whenever the sadness comes over her. Surprisingly, it works. I've even tried it a few times with success. I'm glad Mom told me about this. Perhaps you can try it, too.

I will take charge of my thoughts today.

April 4

Our confusion gives us an opportunity to think awhile longer before we decide what to do.

Are you ever confused about what to do in a certain situation? Mother says it's normal to be uncertain once in a while, but if you get really quiet, your mind will indicate what you should do. I never hear a specific message when I try this, but I do get a feeling about what to do. Mother hears an actual message sometimes. I wish I did.

Last week I went to the teen center with some girls from my neighborhood, and Brittany began making plans for a sleepover that was going to include letting some guys in through her basement window after her parents had gone to sleep. I knew this was going to make my parents mad if they found out. I suggested we not do it. I ended up not getting included. Sometimes doing or saying the right thing isn't appreciated, but it doesn't change it from being right.

I realize pretty quickly what the right thing to do is.

Sadness needs acknowledgment.

When our dog had to be put down, I was really sad. He had been in our family since I was a baby. The veterinarian said he would not get well and this was best for the dog. The whole family felt sad. Mom said we were grieving like when her mother died. Grief is an emotion that needs to be expressed.

Last year Pamela moved away. She had been my best friend since the first grade. For months I was sad about her leaving. We had learned so much together. We wore pantyhose for the first time together. We went to our first movie with boys on the same day. The first time I wore lipstick was when Pamela and I went to a basketball game together. I still miss her. I still think about my grandmother. I'm sure Sassy, our dog, will come into my mind often. You don't forget people or animals who were important to you.

I will cherish my memories today of the special people who are no longer in my life except in spirit.

April 6

Happiness is never more than a moment away.

One of the best ways to make yourself happy is to make someone else happy first. My grandfather said that was why he was happy so often. Every day he gets up and thinks about something he can do for someone else. Sometimes he offers to do the dishes for Grandma. Sometimes he goes over to the neighbor's house to see if he can run an errand for Mr. Jackson, who is in a wheelchair, and many days he writes letters to friends. He says thinking of others is an easy way to ensure your happiness.

I can follow Grandpa's example. I can work diligently on my term paper. This will make Mr. Oshen happy and then me, too. I am determined to do something nice for my mom. Today is her birthday. Making her happy makes our whole family happy because she has a wonderful laugh.

Sometimes happiness comes from doing kind and considerate things for others.

Even though I can't solve your problems, I will be there as your sounding board as long as you need me.

Sandra K. Lamberson

My parents have known each other since they were in second grade. That's more than thirty years. Dad teases Mom and says he knew he was going to marry her the first day he saw her because she had the longest hair of all the girls. She still wears her hair long. I do, too.

I guess you would say they have been friends for a long time. The other night at dinner we talked about friendship. Dad said being a good friend is one of the best gifts you can give someone. It made me wonder if I am as good a friend as I could be. I really like Sara and we enjoy many of the same activities, but I don't always share my thoughts and feelings with her. I do always want what's best for her, and when she does well, I'm happy for her. Dad says this is key to a good friendship.

I want to be a good friend.

April 8

The important lessons in life are seldom obvious.
Robyn Reed

Mr. Grover repeatedly reminds our class that life is full of lessons, and not just the ones we have in school. For one class project, he got two guinea pigs, a male and a female, and before we knew it, the female gave birth to three babies. Mr. Grover used that experience to open our eyes to the consequences of pregnancy and to talk about the importance of not having sex until we're married.

Mr. Grover says we'll experience many lessons, and most of them won't come out of books. As an example, our class couldn't go on a field trip because we were too wild on the bus. That was a tough lesson. Not all of us were that wild. It didn't seem fair that Mr. Grover punished all of us, but he said life isn't always fair and that that's another lesson.

I will have many lessons today, and they all will be important whether I like them or not.

Thanking God can become a habit.

My Sunday school teacher told our class that we should get into the habit of thanking God for every experience we have, even if what has happened doesn't make us happy. I find this hard to agree with. When my bike tire went flat on my way home from Cindy's house, I had to walk the bike for seven blocks. It hardly seems sensible to thank God for that. And when my mother decided she needed a break away from our family for a week, that was no time to say thanks, was it?

Miss Perlman said we don't always know what lesson God has in store for us; that's why we should be thankful. She said in a few hours or days, we will understand the lesson and we will realize we were helped by it. For example, when my bike tire went flat, I remembered that Dad had said I need to check how much air is in the tires before leaving the house. Now I know why. I could have been at Marti's house. She lives two miles away! And when my mom came back, she was so happy to see us again and we appreciated all she does for us.

Saying thank you for everything can be a good habit.

April 10

Wisdom is a quality
we hope to gain as we grow older.

I've been thinking about wisdom lately. To me wisdom means having a deeper understanding of life than the average person. My grandmother is wise. She seems to always have a good answer when I ask a hard question. For instance, when I asked her why there are wars, she said that countries behave like bossy people. Each country wants to have its own way and gets into fights when it can't. She says wars are about people having belief systems that clash.

Wisdom is a strong quality. We probably all hope to have wisdom as we grow older, but it takes a lot of living to become wise. I wonder if I will have as much wisdom as my grandmother. I can learn a lot from her.

I will pay attention today to what older people say.
Maybe I can acquire some of their wisdom.

Difficulties often provide us with unexpected opportunities.

During a history lesson last week, Mr. Groveland said that the struggles we have in life often make us stronger. We were reading about the pioneers and their movement across the country. They had many hardships. Can you imagine going hundreds of miles in a wagon pulled by horses? If you were doing it just for fun, for a few hours, it would be OK. But then I would want to get into a car. How about you?

Mr. Groveland asked each of us to think of a hardship that made us stronger. Samantha remembered when her father left the family. Her mother had a hard time paying the bills. Samantha and her brother had to earn money doing odd jobs for neighbors. That helped Samantha's mom, and Samantha and Nick felt good about it. Samantha said she learned she could do a lot of things she had never tried.

If I'm trying to accomplish something difficult today, I will remember that I'm getting stronger just by trying.

April 12

Perfection can be a goal but not a reality.

I hate to make mistakes. My homework assignment can be covered with smudges because I've had to erase so many mistakes. Mrs. Earl says that mistakes are normal and we learn from them. She doesn't mind the smudges, but she does mind when we forget to turn in the assignment. Last week I tore my math paper while erasing a mistake. I got mad and threw it away.

Being perfect in all things is impossible. Making progress is possible, though. Progress takes practice, lots of it. If you want to play a certain piece perfectly on the piano, you have to practice every day, and you have to concentrate while you're practicing. If your mind begins to think of soccer or the book you're reading during library period, you might make a mistake. But then, being perfect isn't a requirement.

I can practice whatever I want to be good at today.
I will make progress.

Do you know what your destiny is?

Mother says she thinks my destiny is to be a good athlete. I have an aunt who plays on a professional basketball team. Mother says I seem to be strong and fast just like my aunt was when they were children. Destiny is an idea I like to think about. Mother is a scientist for a big company. Did she realize that was her destiny when she did science experiments in high school?

Do you have any idea what your destiny might be? Mom says I'm a little young to know for sure, but the activities we're interested in and good at sometimes indicate what our destiny might be. I'm good at making up stories and I like writing. I might be a novelist someday.

Today is a good day to notice what I am good at.

April 14

Discouragement can easily overtake one's mind.

Do you ever suspect that you will never be successful at a certain activity? Last year I took ballet lessons for a few months, but I could never keep my balance. Brenda, my best friend, was so good. She was the best dancer in our class and she looked great in her costume. I dreaded going to class. Have you ever felt that way about an activity?

I talked over my discouragement with Mom, and she said that everybody gets discouraged occasionally. She told me how hard it was for her to learn to play the flute. She finally gave up because she couldn't make a pretty sound come out. She switched to the piano and had no trouble, at least as long as she was willing to practice. Being discouraged might mean you should switch to another activity. Or maybe it simply means you should practice harder.

If I'm discouraged about something today, I think I will slow down and try a little harder.

Talking to God is always a solution to any problem.

Do you remember to talk to God when something is bothering you? Last year I was visiting my grandmother and heard her talking to herself in the kitchen. When I asked her who she was talking to, she said God. We laughed. She explained that God is always willing to listen and sometimes she needs help in making up her mind. She said she learned to talk to God when she was young.

I have been talking to God ever since. I never hear an exact answer, but Grandma says she just gets a feeling. She doesn't hear a voice, although some people do, she said. What I notice are feelings of comfort or peacefulness, or if I'm trying to make a decision, eventually one choice clearly feels better than another.

If I'm confused about what to do today,
I can always ask God for help.

April 16

The present is all we should pay attention to.

Do you ever miss out on what's going on because you're thinking about how you wrecked your bike yesterday or the speech you have to give tomorrow in class? Keeping my mind on one minute at a time is hard. Every time my mind is somewhere else and not on what's happening, Mom says, I'm missing the "substance of life." I can miss a whole history lesson or not hear an assignment because I'm day-dreaming. I hate it when my sister asks me to go to a movie with her and I'm "somewhere else" in my mind.

Mom says that trying to pay attention to every single thing as it happens is good practice for when I'm older and have a career. That seems like a long way off, but I don't want to miss out on the fun stuff that could be getting ready to happen right now.

I will try to keep my mind on whatever I need to be doing today.

Everyone knows fear.

What are you most afraid of? Everybody is afraid of something. Mr. Howell told us in class yesterday that he was most afraid of getting sick and not being able to teach, because he loves teaching. We went around the room and told what our fears were. I dreaded my turn. I didn't tell the class my real fear. I was afraid they would laugh. I'm afraid of getting picked last when we choose sides for volleyball. I told the class I was afraid of getting Fs on my report card. I've never gotten lower than a C.

Knowing that everyone is afraid of something helps, but I still don't want everyone to know what scares me the most. Mr. Howell says it makes the fear smaller if we share it.

I will try to admit my real fears today to someone I trust.

April 18

Changing your behavior is not hard once you make the decision to do it.

I have a few bad habits. One of the worst is interrupting. My mother gets upset when I do this, which is often. I don't know why I don't seem to notice that she's busy talking already. Mom says it's because I'm thinking about myself and not the person I'm interrupting, and that is being self-centered. She said she thought I "caught" this trait from my dad. We laughed about that, but it is a bad habit.

Bad habits give us something to change. But I can't change them all at once. Mom suggested I pick a couple of them and concentrate on what the opposite behavior might be. The opposite of interrupting is waiting until the person talking is done before I start talking. All I have to do to change that behavior is listen for silence before talking, or really listen to what the person is saying. That doesn't seem too hard, does it?

I'll choose one of my bad habits to work on today.

Sharing our secrets relieves us of a burden.

In my mother's bedroom is a message in a frame that says "Secrets keep us stuck!" When I asked her what this meant, she said we need to share our thoughts and fears with a friend. She has two best friends. One is Dad and the other is Heather. She talks everything over with them. When Dad isn't home or Heather is out of town, then she talks to God. When you keep something inside you, it seems bigger and scarier, she says.

Have you ever had a secret that you were afraid of sharing? I found some money on the coffee table and I put it in my billfold without asking who it belonged to. When Aunt Barbara wondered out loud where her change was, I was too embarrassed to admit I took it. That secret made me feel awful. Finally, I told Mom. She suggested I tell Aunt Barbara. I was scared and ashamed, but Aunt Barbara didn't get mad. I felt so much better after sharing that secret. But not every secret should be shared. For instance, when Dad shows me what he bought Mom for her birthday, I shouldn't tell.

If I am carrying a secret that feels like a burden,
I will choose a safe person to share it with.

April 20

Bossing other people around is fun only for a while.

I sure like to get my way. Everybody likes to be in charge. It's because we all think our way of doing something is best. I see adults do this as much as kids do. I was thinking about this the other day and realized that if we all got our own way, people would never do anything together. We'd all have to do everything alone. That certainly doesn't sound like a fun world, does it?

The solution is to compromise. All your life you will have to compromise with others or you may as well be the only person alive. Through compromise, we learn things we might not learn in any other way. Compromise is what makes it possible for us to grow.

I will try to take turns today. Two people can't each have their own way at the same time.

Change is an absolute.

Everything changes. The trees lose their leaves before winter. Flowers bloom in the spring. The patent leather pumps that I wore to Aunt Lisa's wedding last summer don't fit, nor does my favorite spring jacket. I used to only know easy mathematics, but now I know algebra and some geometry.

Change is part of the passing of time. Mom says change is inevitable; it can't be stopped. It will happen regardless of what you do. Your feet will grow bigger no matter how much you love a certain pair of shoes. Some changes I can accept easily and others are hard for me. Those changes I talk over with Mom or Dad or a friend.

It's good to talk about some of the harder changes in my life.

April 22

Minding your own business is good advice.

I create problems for myself sometimes because I get into other people's business. For instance, when Samantha tries to cheat on an exam, it's not my business to report it. I want to, though. Mom says my reason for wanting to tell is that I don't want her to get away with anything, especially if she ends up with a higher grade.

My parents tell me to mind my own business at home, too, when I start to tell them what my older brother is doing. They don't have to know everything, my dad says, unless someone is about to get hurt. He says this is a good distinction to make every time I want to tell on someone.

If I start to mind someone else's business today, I will think again.

You need to notice and honor your emotions.

Emotions are our feelings. Sadness is a quiet emotion. Anger is a loud emotion. Happiness can be a loud emotion, too, but a very different one from anger. Anxiety is an emotion I feel almost every day. My dad says I am emotional, that I often let whatever is happening get me too riled up. For instance, if my brother teases me, I get upset and yell at him rather than just ignore him. When a friend doesn't include me in an activity, I am afraid that I have no friends left.

Emotions help us to understand who we are. Dad says the healthier we are, the greater variety of emotions we will feel. Someone who is sad all the time might need to see a doctor. Dad said that when he used to be angry all the time, seeing a counselor helped him.

When I listen to my emotions, they have a story to tell me about myself.

April 24

This too shall pass.

Have you heard the phrase, "This too shall pass"? My mother says it at least once a day. She says it when something disturbing is happening. Just yesterday, for instance, she got upset because the refrigerator suddenly quit working. She had to take all our food to the neighbor's house. She called the repairman and he couldn't come out for two or three days. Breakfast and dinner would be hassles for her to prepare. Do you know what she did right after she said, "This too shall pass"? She bought doughnuts for breakfast and ordered pizza for dinner. I liked her solution.

She says it helps to remember that difficult times pass. When we think something bad will last forever, we can become depressed. When we remind ourselves that a better time is around the corner, the burden feels lighter.

Nothing bad lasts forever. I can remember this today.

Some people are molded by their admirations,
others by their hostilities.

Elizabeth Bowen

Does one of your classmates seem to be the most popular? Whether it is a boy or a girl makes no difference. Everyone else always wants that person to be their best friend. In my class Holly is the most popular, and this makes me more than a little envious. Mom suggested I notice how Holly treats others. She said her personality was probably what others liked. I have to admit, Holly is far more generous and kind toward other kids than I often am.

Holly is always nice, especially to the new girls at our school. She includes everybody, and she smiles a lot and seems genuinely happy most of the time. Mom says I can notice the qualities in Holly that I admire and work on developing them myself.

I can consciously strive to develop the traits I admire in others.

April 26

Being helpful doesn't have to take more than a minute of your time.

Every day you have an opportunity to help someone have a better experience. Like yesterday: my friend Trina was working on her term paper for science class and she was upset because a book she needed wasn't in the library. I suggested she look in the encyclopedia. My older brother had taught me how to use it when I was in grade school. She was relieved. She found pages and pages of information she could use.

There are lots of small ways to be helpful. I helped Mom move the yard furniture into the garage when it looked like it was about to storm. The sky was dark and the wind was blowing hard. It never did rain, but she thanked me for helping her, and I felt good doing it.

If I pay attention, I can see many ways to be helpful.

You deserve unconditional love.

Do you ever wonder if your parents really love you? I asked mine recently and they said of course; even if they are upset with me, they still love me. But they don't always like how I behave. Mom reminded me of the time I stayed at Monica's house after telling her I was going to Nicole's. Mom doesn't approve of how Monica's parents think, and she wanted me to choose other friends. Another time she was not happy when I spent my lunch money for the entire week on makeup. They caught me smoking with Brenda once. That was bad, but they still loved me. I haven't smoked since then.

When I was little, my grandfather assured me that God loves us no matter what we do. He told me that God doesn't keep a little black book of our deeds and misdeeds, even though that's what some people think. Knowing that I'm so loved helps me remember that I matter and so do the choices I make.

I will remember how loved I am by my parents and by God.

April 28

Being ignored is hard on adults and kids.

Does it ever seem that no one notices when you arrive for a party? Sometimes at school, I actually feel invisible because I don't get asked to join the girls at the lunch table. Being ignored or left out is painful, isn't it? Mother says that sometimes people don't mean to ignore one another. They just get wrapped up talking to someone and don't notice others approaching. She might be right, but it still feels awful.

She reminded me that I kept playing with all my old friends and hardly even noticed Katrina when she moved into our neighborhood. I'm sure that she felt ignored, but I didn't do it on purpose. I just didn't think about her because I was so busy. Knowing that I've ignored others without intending to means I can assume others might ignore me in the same way.

Am I ignoring someone today? I will pay close attention to my treatment of others.

Disappointments are an important part of life.

I have been disappointed many times lately. I wanted an A on my geography test but didn't get one. I'm not even going to mention the grade I got. And I wanted to get chosen to be a cheerleader. Another disappointment.

My grandmother is wise and believes that whatever comes to us in our lives is a good lesson, regardless of whether we like it or not. Everything that happens is exactly what should happen. This is not easy to understand. Does it mean I needed to get that bad grade and to lose the cheerleading tryouts? And what about when our parakeet flew away?

I can look for the lessons in my disappointments. Mom says that whatever happens will teach me something important.

April 30

Acting responsibly is a sign of adulthood.

I pout when I don't get my way, which is often, and I don't like it when it gets pointed out to me. I think it's a habit I started when I was young and I do it without thinking. Mom says I need to take more responsibility for my behavior and think before doing things. Do you ever get suggestions about your behavior?

To act responsibly takes concentration. Before I answer a question or make a comment to anyone, or before I act, I think through what I will sound like or look like. Mom says this is being aware of the consequences before I create bad ones. Every action and every word spoken have a consequence.

I will be aware of my actions today. They define who I am.

May

Some people think that God
can best be found in nature.

In science class recently, we discussed the life cycle of trees. Mr. Sweeney said that he loved to walk in the woods because it made him feel secure and peaceful. The trees swaying quietly in the breeze made him think of God's quiet presence in his life. Mary raised her hand and asked, "What about the storms that tear through the woods? Where is God then?"

Mr. Sweeney said that he preferred not discussing who or where God was, only that walking through the woods near his home made him appreciate the gentleness of the God he believed in. That turned out to be a lively discussion. My classmates had a lot of opinions about God. Mr. Sweeney said, and I was glad to hear him say it, that everybody has a right to their own beliefs about God.

I like watching the trees sway in the breeze. If I need to feel more peaceful today, perhaps I will take a walk with God.

May 2

Being who you want to be is important.

Are you happy with how you treat your friends? Sometimes I'm mean to Heather and Samantha, like when they have begun a game without including me. I don't know why I act that way, but Mom said that how I behave is always my choice. She said that if I don't like how I'm acting, I'd better choose again.

I daydream about being a doctor when I grow up. I also imagine that I have two children and I have a lot of fun with them. I never see myself, in my mind, being mean like I sometimes am to friends. I think I will start paying more attention to how I'm choosing to behave. If I want my daydreams to come true, I'd better change how I'm acting now.

I will make good decisions today about how I act.

Prayer is a ritual in some families.

I try to remember to say a prayer before falling asleep at night, but I forget sometimes, especially if a friend sleeps over. Then I'm a bit embarrassed to have her know that I pray. Mom said that she and Dad pray before they go to sleep, too. Praying is for everybody who wants to.

Not everybody prays. Mom says prayer helps her feel more peaceful, and then she sleeps better. She worries about my brother and me a lot. She worries about her mother, too, because she's getting old and she fell down and broke her hip. Mother says that praying for all of us helps her to worry less.

I worry about whether my friends will drop me from our group and whether I'll pass all my subjects. Maybe prayer will help me like it helps Mom. I think I'd better study right along with praying, though.

*Praying can help me with a lot of things today.
But I still have to do my part.*

May 4

Your conscience is a good guide.

I have an uncomfortable feeling in my stomach when I've done something rude or thoughtless. My stomach apparently knows right from wrong. Mom says my conscience is bothering me when I've acted badly and that's what makes my stomach upset. Maybe you know this feeling.

There's a way to avoid having an upset stomach. Perhaps when I eat too much pizza (my favorite), I'll still get an upset stomach. But it won't be because of the way I've behaved. Last week I yelled at Rebecca and threatened to ban her from our group because she made me mad. The stomachache I had from this experience could only be blamed on me, not on eating pizza. I can avoid a lot of my stomachaches.

I will feel better if I treat others the way I want them to treat me.

Having a vocation you like is important.

Do you ever daydream about the future, wondering what you'll be when you grow up? I'd like to be an astronomer because I love to watch the stars with my dad. He got his first telescope when he was about my age. He has been interested in stars ever since, although he studied math and became a teacher rather than an astronomer.

Whatever you are interested in might be a clue to what you'll do when you grow up. My mom was interested in playing tennis when she was in high school, but she became a mom rather than a famous tennis player. Her coach in high school was disappointed. I think he wanted her to be famous. But she still plays tennis a lot, and she's teaching me.

My grandmother says it doesn't matter what we end up doing, it's more important how we do it. For instance, my mom loves being a mom: she's energetic, kind, and compassionate.

I will know and develop the things I love to do;
they will help me in life.

May 6

Perfection can be striven for but never gained.
Kathryn Kirkpatrick

Our school motto is "It's progress, not perfection." This is written in big, bold letters across the top of the chalkboard in every classroom. Not every school has a motto, but my parents are glad ours does, because it gives everyone a goal to shoot for. Mom went to a small school in Iowa where the school motto was "All for one and one for all." She said that was a good goal, too. It inspired everyone to help each other as much as possible.

Perfection is not attainable, except for fleeting moments. I get discouraged when I forget this. It's not wrong to attempt to be perfect, of course, but when we fall short of that goal, we need to be understanding of ourselves, not hard on ourselves. The goal is to learn not to be upset by disappointment, to accept it as normal, and to move beyond it. Everyone has had to learn to accept progress in place of perfection.

I may not be perfect today, but I'm good enough.

God is your helper.

Do you ever think about how to respond to someone who has been mean to you? Last week Beth made fun of me during art class because I couldn't get the angle of my drawing correct. The teacher didn't even reprimand her. I felt so humiliated, especially when other kids began to laugh at my work, that I wanted to get her back. I'm glad I remembered what our minister said in church on Sunday. If you're not sure what to say or do in any situation, be quiet for a moment.

I'm sure God isn't going to OK a fight with Beth or anyone else. But maybe I don't have to fight. I only need to do something that makes me feel better in these situations. God can always provide that kind of answer. Mom says she has learned from a group she attends to pray for the people who are mean to her.

I won't act impulsively if someone isn't nice to me today.

May 8

Creativity is a gift everyone has.

I bet you think you aren't good at anything. That's what I used to think, too. I always compared myself with other girls and didn't measure up. The twins were better at science. Of course, their dad is a scientist. Gabriela is better at telling stories. One story that she read about a lame horse made some of us cry. In the third grade, Angie won the spelling bee every Friday for the whole year. No matter how hard I studied, I couldn't outspell her.

I'm a good drummer. I never knew this until we played with instruments during music appreciation month when I was in the sixth grade. The teacher told my parents that I had talent in music. I could keep time without having to count the notes. You never know what talent you might discover you have.

Discovering your creativity makes you feel good.
It's like a dormant flower breaking into blossom.

Hurting others is far too easy.

There are many ways to hurt other people. Saying something mean isn't the only way. Not speaking to a friend can be hurtful. Because it's so easy to hurt others, we have to be careful.

There's really only one way to be careful. It's taking the time to think about what you're doing—before and while you're doing it. Be like a little angel watching over your own shoulder. Notice the look on your face. Listen to the tone of your voice. If someone were talking to you in this way, how would you feel? It can be fun to think of yourself as an angel watching over your shoulder and as yourself, all at the same time. Why not try it?

I can be angelic in all my actions today.

May 10

Change comes in many forms.

People make changes constantly. Many changes are simple, like changing the sheets on the bed or your dirty socks. Some changes are subtle, like when your favorite hairstyle grows out or you suddenly notice the hair on your legs has grown long and looks gross. We often discover these changes by looking in the mirror.

There are other changes far more important. My brother has a bad temper. Dad says he has to change that part of his personality or he'll end up having no friends. My mother keeps saying she needs to change how she eats because she's gained ten pounds.

I'm sure I have some changes I need to make. For instance, I keep daydreaming about the guy who moved here last summer. I have gotten a failing grade in history twice in the past month because of daydreaming at the wrong time.

If I'm not having fun today, maybe it's because some kind of change is necessary.

How we think determines
what we receive from our experiences.

Your thoughts are important. This seems like a simple idea, but it can be tricky. For instance, let's say you're staring at Katie, the smallest girl in your gym class, and thinking, "What a shrimp! How can she help our basketball team?" If those are your thoughts, you will not be kind to her. Because your thoughts are far from friendly, your behavior won't be either.

Another example: if you're taking a test and your mind is on the argument your parents had during breakfast, you won't hear the questions and you could fail. Thoughts take up important space in our minds. You can't think of two things at once. The thought that's there takes charge of your behavior. It's something to think about, isn't it?

I will be aware that whatever is in my mind
will influence what I do.

May 12

Positive qualities visit
even the most unlikely candidate.

Ruth Atchley

Every person has many good qualities. For instance, Angela is good at ice skating because she's coordinated and has good balance. She'll probably be on the hockey team in senior high. My mother is friendly and happy most of the time. Dad says that's her best quality, the one that won his heart. Her ability to bake great pies is a good quality, too!

It's easy to notice others' good qualities and harder to notice my own. If I take the time, though, and look at what I like about me and my life, I can come up with a list. I have good friends, special talents, and a loving family. I'm a lot of fun, I study hard, and I'm pretty good at sports.

I will watch closely today for my good qualities.

Confidence in ourselves can be planted, watered, and grown.

Having confidence is believing that you can do something without needing the constant reassurances of others. My mother has confidence in her ability to drive a car. She learned through driver's education classes when she was young and she's careful every time she drives. My father is confident that he'll get another promotion at work because he went back to college for more education.

My older sister says she has confidence that she'll get into the college she wants to because she has studied hard throughout high school and made good grades. Do you have confidence that you can do something well, or do you need other people to tell you this?

I would like to have confidence that I can do some things well today.

May 14

Equality exists in diverse forms.

My friend Pam is so cute. Her hair curls just the way I want mine to curl, but, of course, it won't. Brittany gets an A in math on every test! No matter how hard I try, I miss one or two problems. Mom says it's because I'm careless. When I think of these two people I see every day, it's hard to believe that we're equal. They seem better in so many ways.

Mom says being equal doesn't mean we're alike. She says we're born with different looks and abilities, but no one's abilities or looks make them more important to God and our universe. Everybody is different in some ways but equal in value in every way. This is not so easy to understand, but it will make more sense as I grow older.

I am as important as everyone I can see. I'm not better than others—I'm equal to others.

Confidence is the opposite of nervousness.

Some mornings I wake up feeling nervous. I can't eat breakfast on those mornings. Mom says she gets nervous, too. She suggested I write about my feelings in my journal. She bought me one for my thirteenth birthday. She said that writing in a journal helps her whenever she has a problem.

I feel lucky that Mom shared the idea about a journal with me. It means I don't have to stay nervous. I always feel better if I write awhile. Another thing that helps is to see if God has any ideas for me. Sometimes those come to me while I'm writing.

If I'm feeling nervous, I can talk to my mom or dad or write in my journal, and I will feel more sure of myself.

May 16

Setting goals is a good habit to develop.

Do you set goals? In other words, do you make a plan for the future and then figure out all the steps to make the plan happen? Most important of all is to do the steps, of course. My dad says lots of people have goals but they don't accomplish them. He used my uncle as an example. Uncle Jeff has started college three times but he never goes more than a few months. He'll never graduate that way. I sometimes wonder if graduation is really his goal.

My soccer coach says it's wonderful practice to start having goals when we're young because we'll make more of our lives if we master this skill now. One of my soccer goals is to be able to make the girls' team in high school. I made the middle school team. That's a beginning. I'm on my way.

I can have many kinds of goals. Goals help me shape my life.

Everybody loves praise.

Recognition for having done a good job, no matter what the job, is important. I feel better if Mom notices I've done something as simple as cleaning up the mess in my bedroom. I'm proud when Miss Barkley reads one of my short stories to our English class. She thinks it's good or that wouldn't happen. I especially like it when my dad praises me, because he usually doesn't say a lot.

I feel a little bit taller whenever I get praised for something. Does that seem strange to you? It feels nice to praise someone else for something they've done. I wonder if Holly feels a little bit taller when I tell her how lucky she is to play the piano so beautifully. Praise is a wonderful thing. It makes everyone, the one who gets it and the one who gives it, feel better.

An easy way to feel better today is to praise someone else for something they've done.

May 18

Criticism seldom feels good
but it may be necessary.

Thelma Kirkpatrick

How does it make you feel when you are criticized? My brother doesn't seem to mind, but I do. Especially when I get criticized at school, I feel embarrassed. Last week Mr. Nye told me that I spent far too much time talking to Josh, the new boy who sits next to me in science class. Of course, all of the kids started to tease me, saying Josh must be my boyfriend. Actually, my science test scores have gone down since he moved here.

When Mom criticizes me for not remembering to do my chores, I don't feel embarrassed, but I often feel ashamed. She works so hard at her job and when I don't help her, she has more work to do and that's not fair.

If I'm criticized today, I will assume I need to look closer at what I'm doing.

Apologizing may be the next right thing in my list of things to do today.

Are you willing to apologize when you've done something you know is wrong? I have a hard time with this. Just last week my dad was upset because I spilled brown paint on the driveway while trying to cover up the burn marks on my dresser. Heather and I had been smoking in my bedroom, and we'd set the cigarettes on the edge of the dresser top. I figured I could paint over the burn marks. Spilling the paint attracted attention, and my dad found out about the burn marks. One apology wasn't enough, if you know what I mean!

I was really ashamed. I didn't leave my room for a while. I couldn't figure out how to make Dad trust me again. He said I had better learn two things: how to make apologies more quickly in the future, and how to refrain from behavior that I know doesn't meet with his approval. I will never smoke again.

I may need to apologize to someone today.
I hope I'm quick to do it.

May 20

Laughter is by definition healthy.

Doris Lessing

My grandfather told me that I don't laugh enough. Mom agreed that I'm serious for someone my age, but she said the important thing is for me to enjoy my life and the activities I'm in. She said maybe my laughter was more inside than outside. I smile to myself often, like when I'm watching TV or reading a book or watching my little sister trying to feed herself.

When I told Grandpa that my laughter was on the inside more than the outside, he chuckled, and said that he was glad I laughed, wherever I did it. He didn't laugh much when he was young after his father died. He had to get a job selling newspapers to help pay for the groceries. When he grew up, he found it hard to have fun until he met my grandmother. He said he wanted to make sure that I didn't miss out on fun like he had.

I will find plenty of reasons to laugh today if I look for them.

Hope gives you something to do
when worry is filling your mind.

JoAnn Elliott

I hope for many things. For one thing, I hope I have enough money for college someday. Right now my biggest hope is that my older sister comes home. She left three weeks ago and said she would call us when she was ready.

Mrs. Glasco, my favorite teacher since grade school, seems happy all the time, and she says her happiness is because she never gives up hope that everything will turn out for the best. Mom agrees. She says that everything always turns out like it should, even something as difficult as my sister moving away. I can hope that the relationship between my sister and my parents improves. I can also hope that my sister knows how much I love her.

Everything will work out, even if I can't see how yet.

May 22

Saying no to using drugs and drinking isn't as easy as it sounds.

I want to set a good example for my younger sisters. My parents want me to, also. But drugs and alcohol seem to be everywhere. And sometimes they look like fun. But that's not always the case. I have a cousin who is twenty-five who can't hold down a job and hasn't even finished college. He started to use drugs and drink in high school and hasn't been able to stop.

I want to do many things with my life. I don't want to waste it. My teacher says there are tons of ways to say no. "Be inventive!" he says. I'm glad I have friends who want to play sports, study, and make plans for an exciting life. They help me make good decisions.

I hope I will have the courage to do the right thing.

People can inspire us
to change how we think and act.

Have you ever had a friend who seemed to make you feel good just by being around you? My science lab partner is like that. Not only is she smart, she's polite and nice to all the kids in class. She always tries to figure out a way to include everybody in class activities. And she never makes fun of anyone. I envy her. My mother says she's an inspiration to all of us.

My great-grandmother is an inspiration to a lot of people in the way that she keeps learning new skills even in her old age. She is seventy-eight, and last year she took a college course to learn to speak Spanish. Now she can talk to her new neighbors who don't speak much English.

Mom says that inspiring others is nothing more than continuing to live your life productively and kindly. We can all do that.

I can be an inspiration to someone today.

May 24

Wanting to be liked can result in trouble if I make it too important.

We all want to be liked. Sometimes to be liked I do things I wouldn't ordinarily do. I'm mean to a friend because the other girls are, or I make fun of my teacher even though I like him. I do it to get a laugh or approval from my friends.

The truth is that laughter or approval is short-lived but my regret about how I acted lasts longer. One time I got in real trouble and was sent to the principal's office. That experience made me realize how my need to be liked, if I let it be too important, can overshadow my values. This could get me into even more trouble if the kids around me are drinking or using drugs.

I need to be clear about what the right choice is for me. I'm strong enough to put this first and the need to be liked second.

Knowing what we need to know
when we need to know it, and not before,
is what is best for us.

Do you ever wish you knew exactly what was going to happen when you grow up? I often wonder if I'll get married and have children. My sister claims she never wants to have kids. I wonder if I'll be a doctor like my mom or in sales like my dad. My parents say I can probably be whatever I want to be if I'm willing to work hard for it.

Mom's philosophy is that it's best if we don't know the future until it begins to happen. She said that some things that happen would upset us too much if we knew about them ahead of time. She reminded me of the car accident my grandparents had. They weren't seriously hurt, but if they had known it was going to happen, they would have been terrified. Mother assured me that we always know what we need to know when the time is right.

Today will happen however it should, I guess.

May 26

Anger is a thorn on the rosebush of life.

Anger is like a thorn on a rosebush. Along with all of life's beauty and gifts, there are things that make me angry. My mom says no to something I want to do; all my friends are at Sara's and nobody called me; my little brother got into my paints again. What a mess he made.

If I don't talk about my anger, I become crabby and pick on everybody around me. Sometimes I say I hate my mom or my little brother. My mom always stops me and says, "That's not OK, but it is OK to be angry." When I talk about it, to Mom or a friend, I begin to feel better. Then some of the air goes out of my anger balloon.

If I'm angry today, I will talk my feelings over with someone I can trust.

Feeling invisible isn't any fun.

While in a group of friends, have you ever begun to wonder if your friends just cannot see you? Mom says this happens to everybody. Certain girls are often the center of attention and when you're never that girl, it's easy to begin to think the group doesn't even know you're around. It helps to know that everyone feels this way sometimes, because it often seems like you're the only one who's being ignored. Some girls are just more assertive and "visible" than other girls.

Being assertive means taking the risk to speak up more frequently. It means that others might disagree with you. This isn't always fun, and when it happens, you might wish you could fade into the background, be more invisible. It is important to find a balance between assertiveness and being quiet. Mom says that with practice, I will figure it out.

My friends and I can take turns being the center of attention.

May 28

Every moment is a gift from God.

My grandfather is trying to help me appreciate each experience in my life. He says he learned this lesson so late in his life and missed a lot because he was somewhere else in his mind when the good things were happening. For example, he said that when his first child, my dad, was born, he was so worried about something at work that he was on the phone and not even in the room with Grandma. He is still sorry about that because my dad was his only child.

Grandpa lives with us and reminds me every day to look and listen when others are talking and playing around me. He thinks God puts us in particular places to learn and have fun with certain people. He may be right. I've learned a lot of soccer tricks from Amanda.

I will remember to notice everything and everyone close to me today.

We are rich only through what we give,
and poor only through what we refuse.
Anne-Sophie Swetchine

Generosity is an important idea. Miss Sable, my favorite teacher, says generosity can mean giving things away, like splitting my candy bar at lunch with Tanya, or sharing my favorite things with a girlfriend at a sleepover. Generosity can mean having a big heart. For example, it can mean not staying mad at a friend for a long time even when she has gossiped about you. Being willing to forgive someone even though they hurt you is being generous in an important way.

When I was younger I thought being generous meant you had to give someone money. Now I know it can mean giving lots more than that. My grandmother believes that being generous in other ways is even more important. I think she's right. Don't you?

I can be generous in many ways today.

May 30

Continuous effort—not strength or intelligence—
is the key to unlocking your potential.

Liane Cordes

Do you know what it means to persevere? Our parents and our teachers have asked us to do this, but they probably used another word for it. To persevere means to keep trying until we master a technique or complete a project that we have put off. Cleaning my closet is one of those projects. Learning something new in mathematics may take perseverance because we often don't understand the new formulas at first. Continuing to work on the new method makes it understandable eventually.

Many things in life need our perseverance. Learning to be polite and kind takes practice, and for my older brother, lots of it. So does learning to listen. We often think we're listening, but our minds wander to how our outfit compares with the outfits of the other girls in the class, or to the trip we're planning to take over the holidays. "Perseverance" is a good word for our vocabulary, and a necessary quality for our lives.

Today will give me a chance to know that I have learned the meaning of perseverance.

What a strange pattern the shuttle of life can weave.
Frances Marion

Some people believe that every single thing that happens is part of a big design created by God, or some supreme being, on our behalf. My dad questions this idea but believes that we can learn from everything that happens, even disasters. He recalled the earthquake that hit California a few years ago. He said that many people who had been strangers before the quake became friends because so many of them needed help. Many people reached out and offered help to others.

It may seem absurd to think that a disaster can be an opportunity for good, but we can point to thousands of ways we have seen this happen. Here's one: My grandmother's house caught fire when she was a young single mother, trying to raise my mother and her three sisters. When the firefighters came, one of them took an interest in her misfortune, and they fell in love. He became my grandfather. Something good came out of that disaster. Can you think of some examples from your life?

I think these unexpected "miracles" happen often. It helps to remember that there is something good to be found even in a difficult situation.

June

That which is surrendered is taken care of best.
Marianne Williamson

What does being peaceful mean to you? Does it mean being happy? If so, I am generally peaceful on Saturdays when I don't have school. My grandmother talks about "being at peace." Is that different from being peaceful? She said that when my grandfather died, he was at peace at last. Surely that didn't mean he was happy to be dead. Mom says Grandmother was happy that his struggle was over. He had been sick and courageous for a long time.

A book I read last week talked about feeling calm and quiet inside. Miss Haverly, the librarian at school, says that feeling peaceful often means feeling quiet and an inner softness.

Although it is sometimes exciting to feel stirred up inside, I would like to feel peaceful at least part of every day.

June 2

How we think determines our actions.

Last week our geography class was studying the Egyptians. It was amazing that they could build the pyramids many centuries ago. Scientists aren't sure how they did it. But one thing is certain, they must have had a strong belief in themselves to have been able to accomplish that feat. How we think about ourselves is important. People can accomplish so much when they think they can.

This is true of every person's life, not just of the Egyptians or the person who becomes president of the United States. It is true of you and me. Here is how it worked for me last week. I was feeling shy when I went to Maria's birthday party because I was the only one invited from our class. But all the way there, I coached myself to introduce myself to the first person I came to in the room. Guess what? Monica and I became friends right away, and then meeting everyone else felt easy.

My thinking is a lot more important than I realize.

Fear is a common emotion.

What are you most afraid of? I asked my great-grandfather this question, and he said he was afraid he would miss out on something important that was being said to him because of his tendency to daydream. That seems like a strange fear to me. I like to daydream. When I told Mom what he said, she was impressed. She thought it explained why he was still so lively at the age of ninety-one.

If I had to answer my own question, I would say I'm afraid of not having friends. Being lonely is not fun. That was how I felt when I first moved to Chicago from Atlanta. None of the girls seemed to notice me for the longest time, not until I started inviting a few at a time to my house. Brad, my brother, says he's afraid of not getting into college. He doesn't have to worry because he studies hard.

Our fears teach us a lot about ourselves. I'm glad they don't have to last forever. We can let go of a fear by changing how we think and behave. For instance, my great-grandfather looks closely at the person speaking to him, and he immediately asks a question or sums up what was said. He doesn't miss much this way.

I can overcome my fears rather than being overcome by them.

June 4

Being hopeful is far more helpful than being discouraged.

Probably a dozen times a day, I hope something will happen. For instance, yesterday I hoped that I would pass the history exam. I will find out next week. Last week I hoped that Carole would invite me to her birthday party. I was disappointed when she didn't, but I thought she wouldn't. My parents keep hoping that they will win the lottery. My grandmother said that money never makes anyone happy for long. She said they should hope for good health instead.

Having hope, even when things don't work out as you'd like, feels better than constant worry. When I'm hopeful about something, my attitude is generally pleasant. Some adults say that a pleasant attitude often invites good things to happen. Maybe when I'm pleasant, the other people around me actually help my wishes come true. My dad says our expectations for positive things can sometimes draw what we expect to us. He says the opposite can be true, too.

I will monitor my thoughts today.

Blaming others can be a bad habit.

Do you try to blame others for mistakes you made? My mother says I do this too often. Let me explain what happened yesterday and you decide if it was actually my fault. Dana, Chad, and I were playing catch in Dana's backyard. Just for fun, Chad started to throw the ball high and sometimes too hard for Dana to catch. She kept asking him to play fair, but he wouldn't. I felt sorry for Dana and started throwing the ball hard at Chad. On my last throw, he jumped aside and the ball went through Mr. Hathaway's kitchen window. Mr. Hathaway came running out and was mad. I quickly tried to explain and blamed Chad, of course. All Mr. Hathaway kept asking was, "Who threw the ball?"

I can't deny that I threw the ball. Mom says that is the only thing I need to pay attention to. Life isn't always fair, and I did break the window. Not blaming Chad or someone else when something goes wrong isn't always easy.

I will not blame others for my mistakes today.

June 6

Daydreaming can be productive.

Do you have trouble keeping your mind on your homework? I didn't used to, but ever since we started studying about the African culture in geography class, that's all I think about. I get the funny feeling that I used to live in Africa eons ago. I know that can't be possible, but my mind wanders to the people and their habits even when I'm in the middle of a geometry lesson or a science assignment. I can almost hear their voices murmuring to me.

Dad says I have an overly active imagination. I don't like to upset him, but I love the dreams my mind makes up. Maybe I can set aside some time every day to dream all I want, but put the dreams aside when other work needs to be done. Maybe I could put this interest I have into an extra credit project.

Daydreams can be wonderful as long as I set them aside when there is other work to do.

Attitude is everything.

Our principal picks an idea for everyone in our school to focus on a week at a time. She announces the idea on the intercom first thing every Monday morning. This week she chose "Attitude is everything." My homeroom class discussed this for a few minutes before the bell rang. Mr. Simpson asked all of us to keep track of our attitudes all day and be ready to talk about it in homeroom at the end of the day. We really got into our discussion.

Ryan, the new boy in homeroom, said he was angry in his first-hour class because he forgot his assignment. He stayed mad all day and got a low grade on the history quiz, too. He learned that his attitude had messed up his whole day. Betsy said she was so happy at having gotten an A+ on her report that she had fun all day. Mr. Simpson said we had gotten the right idea about the importance of attitude.

I intend to notice my attitude constantly today.

June 8

Prayer can change lives.

My family has begun to say grace before the evening meal. We never used to pray before eating, but my grandmother moved in with us because she is too old to live alone, and she asked if we could say grace. My little sister always gets the giggles for some reason. My dad seems a bit uncomfortable, too. Mom shared that she prays many times during a day, and she said she thought it helped her day in many ways.

I pray every time I have a test in school, but I don't get good grades on all of them. Mom says prayer doesn't really work that way. Her prayers are for being at peace. That way she can handle whatever is happening in her life. Maybe I should try her kind of prayer. What do you pray for?

I will pray to feel peaceful today and to be able to handle whatever comes my way.

Opportunities are our invitations for change.

Do you take advantage of the opportunities that come your way? My parents believe that every situation can be seen as an opportunity to experience something important. Just a few months ago, Dad lost his job because his company moved his division to another city. We could have moved, but it would have meant Mom giving up her job and that didn't seem fair to her. Instead of being upset, Dad said a new door must be opening for him in another company. Even before finding the job, he was excited about what the new job might be.

Seeing every situation, no matter how upsetting, as an opportunity for something new in your life is quite a change from how our neighbor thinks. He's always growling. He's never happy, no matter what's happening. I think my parents' philosophy is much better.

I wonder what my opportunities will be today?

June 10

Being impulsive can cause unnecessary trouble.

"Quit being so impulsive!" Some days I hear this a zillion times. I wasn't even sure what it meant the first time my mom said it, but because she had raised her voice, I knew it wasn't good. The tone of her voice sent me to the dictionary. Acting before thinking something through is more or less the definition, and it's a habit I am guilty of.

When I was in the first grade, a new family moved in next door. There was a girl about my age. I noticed right away that her bike didn't have training wheels. I got my older brother to take mine off and then jumped on the bike at the top of the hill by our house. The next thing I knew, I was racing out of control down the hill. I didn't make it to the bottom upright, and I ended up with a broken ankle. I hadn't even realized that I had to learn about balance first. Just because Hanna and I were the same size didn't mean I was ready to ride a bike. Sometimes I'm impulsive in what I do and in what I say.

Thinking first is always a good idea.

If you don't have confidence,
the good news is that you can develop it.

Having confidence can make every part of one's life easier. I'm pretty confident that I can master the history lesson and pass the test. I have a good memory. I'm confident that I'll get chosen for a team when we play ball after school because I run fast and am a good catcher. My dad hopes I'll make the girl's softball team when I get into high school. But I'm not confident about playing piano in front of my cousins. They are so good.

I sometimes lack confidence in my ability to make friends, too. My stepdad worried about the same problem, and he said his adviser suggested that he notice how others seemed to make friends. I've noticed that Pamela is popular with all our classmates. She seems to be everyone's best friend. She's polite and tries to include other kids in all her activities. Maybe I should try to practice her behavior along with practicing the piano.

I am glad for the confidence I have. I will work on developing it in other areas.

June 12

If there were no others to share ourselves with,
life would be meaningless.

Carlotta Posz

My little brother and I fight all the time, but then he'll share something with me or I will with him and it feels good. When my family picked me up from camp after a week, I realized how much I missed his voice and his goodnight hugs. He held my hand most of the way home.

Whenever my mom bakes cookies, she sends some over to Mrs. Johnson, the widow up the street. Mrs. Johnson always buys some plants from me when our school sells them. Our soccer coach sells cosmetics and often passes out bath salts to us after a hard game. My dad and I read to each other on weekend nights.

Sometimes it feels like all these gestures create a web of lace around me, a web of caring and kindness I can lean into whenever I need to.

The web of people around me gives my life meaning.

Anger can be expressed in thoughtful ways.

Thinking about what I want to say before expressing my anger is a good habit. It has saved me from being grounded many times. I learned this from my dad's new wife, Anita. I don't see her often, but the last time she came along when I met Dad for dinner, I had just had an ugly argument with Rebecca, my best friend. Anita said that she had a bad temper when she was a girl. Her grandmother had told her to count to ten before saying a word when she was mad. She said it calmed her down. Often she even got over being mad.

I feel awkward being quiet when someone is yelling at me, but I learned that it works. Just last week I was mad at Mom because she made me pick up after Kevin. He had made a mess and should have cleaned up after himself. Pausing before saying a word saved me from getting into real trouble. What I hadn't known was that Kevin was sick and had gone to bed. I am glad I didn't argue.

Instead of losing my temper, I will count to ten.

June 14

We all have character defects.

Do you know what a character defect is? A character defect can be a behavior that is harmful to our relationships with others. For instance, I get into trouble with my parents because I interrupt when they're trying to explain things to me. This is a character defect. Smarting off to my younger sister is a character defect, too, at least in my family.

I've noticed that many of my friends have character defects. Jennifer often walks away in the middle of our conversation. That's rude. But worse than that, Thomas constantly picks on the smaller kids on the playground. They often run away, crying out of fear, and then he laughs. Some defects appear worse than others, but my mother says comparing our own defects with those of others and then deciding ours are not as bad can be a defect, too.

I will focus on just one defect today and make a promise to myself not to show it in my behavior.

Kindness can be a strong antidote for bitterness.

Our neighbor is a bitter man. Mom says that ever since his wife died, he has lost his sense of humor and has closed himself off from others. He reacts negatively to all his neighbors and refuses to join in any block activities. His bitterness verges on being dangerous to others. Just last week, he almost hit Mindy, my youngest sister, when she wandered into his yard to chase a butterfly. She was scared, and my dad was shocked that a grown man could act like that with a child.

We all thought that my dad was going to challenge Mr. Nolan to a duel. You could see my mother's concern on her face. She suggested that she would go over to Mr. Nolan's house and share her disappointment over how our relationship with him had changed. She said that treating him mean would make matters worse. She thought his actions were just because he was lonely. Mother is always looking for a kind way to respond to others.

If I am not feeling kind, I will try to think of ways to act with kindness.

June 16

Giving up the need to control isn't easy,
but it's so rewarding!

Are you often preoccupied with making others play a game your way, and they just won't go along? An "incorrigible controller"—that's how my stepmother describes me. The main problem is that it doesn't work very well. Others aren't likely to go along with your plan unless that is exactly what they have already decided to do.

This has been a challenging lesson. My way of doing anything always seems best. My friends might agree that my way is best sometimes. The rest of the time they prefer another way. Mom says she has so much more time to laugh since she quit trying to control everyone else. She suggested I try it, but it's not easy.

I will try to remember that I don't have the right to control how others do anything. I am only in charge of me.

Each person sees things a little differently.

"Perspective" means how you choose to see or interpret a situation or experience. We talked about perspective in class last week. It has been on my mind since. I have made it a point to notice how differently the people in my family interpret particular situations. Mr. Hamilton had suggested we do this as an experiment. Here is an example.

My older sister had applied to a college in another state. Dad had warned her that her grade point average was low and not to be disappointed if she was not accepted. She didn't seem worried. Last week the big letter came. We were all excited for her to get home from school. When she arrived, she seemed reluctant to open the letter in front of us. Her mood became solemn, and she seemed almost self-conscious about us knowing the verdict. Mother interpreted this as fear. Dad saw it as secretiveness. I just figured she was sure we would make fun of her if she was turned down. See how different our perspectives were? Mr. Hamilton was right. Seldom do we see any situation the same way another person sees it.

Taking notice of how my friends see our experiences today could be educational.

June 18

Friendship of a kind that cannot easily be reversed tomorrow must have its roots in common interests and shared beliefs.

Barbara W. Tuchman

My grandmother says that nothing is more important than our friendships. She thinks that the members of our family should be considered our best friends. I'm not sure I agree with that part, particularly when it comes to my brother Ryan. He is a pain in the neck. But I am thrilled with having so many fabulous friends. The reason they are so important, she says, is because each one of them has something specific to teach us. They help us make good decisions about our lives.

I was skeptical. I couldn't think of one thing I had learned from Lisa. She seemed too quiet to teach anybody anything. When I asked Grandma about this, she said Lisa was a good listener and listening is one of the most important lessons for any of us to learn. What I'm learning from Teresa is more obvious. She works diligently on everything she pursues. I've learned how to be more diligent just being around her. I wonder what my friends learn from me? Grandma says I should be more conscious of how I act in front of them. That will show me what I teach them.

Friendships will help guide me through life.

Defensiveness is related to fear.

Whenever I make a suggestion to my friend Kim, she gets defensive, which means she always has an excuse for why she does something her way. Defensive people tend to get irritated by the suggestion that they try a new way. They see the suggestion as criticism. I remember my fifth-grade teacher telling our class that when someone gets defensive, it usually means they are afraid. When I make a suggestion to Kim, I do it nicely. Why would she be afraid?

I need to remember how I react when someone makes a suggestion to me. If I'm honest, I would have to say I get a little annoyed. I don't like to be wrong. In fact, I generally think everyone should do everything my way. When I get defensive, I realize it is because I don't want to be wrong. Am I afraid of appearing as though I don't always have the right way of doing something?

If I find myself being defensive, I will look for whatever is behind it.

June 20

I am learning who I am, and I like me!

Liking yourself is one of the most important things you can achieve in life. Mr. Dorling, my social studies teacher, brought this up for discussion after an incident in our school that upset many of us. Some older kids trashed the bathrooms during the school festival. Mr. Dorling said that people who like themselves do not behave this way. He said a person needs to learn who they are to be able to change whatever behaviors they need to change.

I've noticed that I'm willing to help Mom at home after she gets off work. I love to help the younger kids learn to read. I get the chance to do that at least once a week, generally on Fridays. Liking how I am with others is a good indication that I like myself. I doubt that I will ever want to do the kind of thing those other kids did at the school festival.

I like my good qualities.

Believing in God makes sense to millions of people.

My family goes to church every Sunday. Most of the time we say grace before our evening meal. Mother seldom has to remind me to have a little conversation with God before going to sleep. When I was small she taught me that God could be considered my friend and daily companion. God was with me wherever I went. I used to imagine God walking beside me. I still do that when I remember to.

Not every family goes to church. Mother says not every person believes in God, but that I should treat everyone I meet in a loving way regardless of what their beliefs are. Other people don't have to believe in God just because our family does. Some people don't like to share what their religious beliefs are. I love to talk about God. God has helped my family so many times. It's interesting that we are not all alike.

My beliefs are mine. Others don't have to share them.
I can honor my own beliefs and others' as well.

June 22

Harmony in a family helps it function better.

Being in harmony with others is important. I got a better idea of what being in harmony means when we discussed it last year in social studies class. Here is how it works. In most of our discussions with others, we do not agree on a lot of things. In fact, we seldom see a situation in the same way, even when we're standing side by side observing it. My mother says even the primary colors look different to our eyes.

You can be in harmony when you have so many differences if you decide to peacefully let every person see and feel however they want to. You know this isn't easy if you've ever tried it, but I'm so much happier when I'm not arguing with a friend or someone in my family about our differences. Mr. Hamilton said that if all the countries in the world decided it was OK to have differences, we could avoid wars. Wouldn't that be wonderful?

At least I know I can avoid a war in my own small life today.

The forgiving state of mind
is a magnetic power for attracting good.
Catherine Ponder

When I have angered my mom or stepdad, I'm not comfortable. I watch them to see if they've gotten over their anger. I can usually tell by the look on their faces when they glance at me. If they smile, I feel like I've been forgiven.

To be forgiven is important, isn't it? It changes how both people feel, almost instantly. When Mom has forgiven me, I feel relieved, and she says that she feels relieved, too. Being angry makes her feel heavy, she says.

It works the same way for me when I'm angry at a friend or someone in my family. Yesterday I was mad at Rosie for borrowing my bike and then leaving it at the park. She had locked it, but still, it was there and I was at home. Until I forgave her, I couldn't enjoy anything else I was doing. My mind just hung on to the anger. Forgiveness changes how we feel inside.

Forgiveness is essential in good relationships.

June 24

Letting go is an important part of life.

How hard is it for you to let a friend be however she wants to be? For instance, my friend Jessica is always whining about something. No matter what we're doing, she wants to do it some other way. And the harder she tries to change my mind, the more I dig in. Do you know what I mean? I just don't like someone to try to control me. I want them to let go!

Mom says I need to practice this myself. She said that she observes me doing the same thing with Mindy, my younger sister, that Jessica does to me. I do always think my way is best. Being able to let go of what someone else does is not easy. Mom says that if I can remember that we need others' opinions to grow in new directions, it will help me. I need to practice this skill. How about you?

I will not try to change a single other person today.

Mistakes are no big deal if they are acknowledged.

I hate making mistakes that are obvious to others, like when I shout out a wrong answer when the teacher is holding up flash cards. It seems like I'm better at the algebra we're learning than the division tables I learned a couple of years ago. In fact, I didn't learn them well at all.

It's normal to be wrong once in a while. My dad says he has made mistakes at work many times, and the important lesson is to learn from them. A big one he made was leaving out an important step when he was setting up his new computer. It meant he had to start over, but he learned a bunch of additional steps he wouldn't have learned otherwise. Mistakes can sometimes be our best teachers.

If I make a mistake today, I will simply correct it and not worry over it.

June 26

At times fear grips me and
I can concentrate only on the anxiety.

Michele Fedderly

What makes you most afraid? We talked about this in my family last night. My sister had been chased by a bunch of older kids when she was coming home from a friend's house. It was getting dark and she was scared, especially when she heard them call her by name and she didn't know a single one of them. She said her heart was pounding. She recognized another friend's house and ran up to the door and knocked as hard as she could. They let her in, and she called my mom for a ride.

My parents agreed she did the right thing. My dad said that if the same thing ever happened to me or Joey, we should run up to a house where there is a light and ask for help. This has never happened, but I've been afraid at night because I thought I saw a shadow cross my room. I have a lamp close to my bed, and I often turn it on.

It's good to know that at times when I feel afraid
there are always safe, comforting people I can turn to.

Acceptance of each day's challenges and gifts is worth striving for.

My mom says I spend too much time wanting to be older or someplace that I am not. I envy my sister. She gets to drive the car, and she can stay out late with her boyfriend. She doesn't have to help clean up after dinner anymore because she has a job after school at the library. It doesn't seem fair. My brother and I have more work now.

Mom's general response to my complaint is that I am just where I need to be. I'm not sure I understand this, but she says we are always "in the right place at the right time." She says this is her philosophy. We each have certain things we need to learn, and wherever we are is where we need to be to learn them. This keeps her satisfied rather than always wishing to be somewhere else. It might be to my advantage to adopt her philosophy. What do you think of this idea?

I can be happy where I am or I can complain. It's up to me.

June 28

What you praise you increase.

Catherine Ponder

Being praised by my homeroom teacher last week for my ideas in a class discussion and by my dad for being honest about smoking a cigarette I had found made me feel good. In fact, any time someone tells me they like what I have done or said, or that they think I'm kind or helpful, I feel good. I think everyone likes praise.

Maybe I could offer praise to my brothers and sisters and friends more often. Wouldn't it be nice if every person in the universe felt appreciated? Maybe I can start a trend by offering praise to people close to me, and they in turn, because they feel so good about receiving praise, might offer it to the next person they see.

I will look for opportunities to praise someone today.

Our expectations can become our reality.

JoAnn Reed

Do you remember reading the book about the little engine that said, "I think I can, I think I can, I think I can," and then climbed the mountain? I remember feeling happy for the little engine. Mother told me how important it is to believe you can do something in order to actually do it. She said that when she took skiing lessons as a young girl, she was positive she would never master the turns. Because she was so sure she couldn't do it, she didn't learn them the first year. The second winter she tried skiing, her dad reminded her about the little engine that could. She said it changed how she felt about the challenge.

Mother says believing in ourselves is mandatory, which means we must do it. It's mandatory that we go to school until the age of sixteen. It's mandatory that we pass a driver's exam before we can get a license to drive a car. It's mandatory that we wear a shirt and shoes before we enter most stores and restaurants. It's mandatory that we believe in ourselves if we want to succeed in any effort.

I like the idea that believing I can accomplish something makes it more likely that I can.

June 30

Doubt is a common feeling.

Do you ever doubt that you can get an A on an exam? Or do you ever doubt that other girls like you? These are two of my doubts. I'm glad we talked about our doubts in school the other day, because I soon realized that my doubts were pretty much like everyone else's.

What makes us doubt ourselves? Mrs. Petros says doubt and faith are opposites. She says that when she has faith that things will work out, they usually do. When she doubts, something often goes wrong. She suspects that doubt triggers the very thing we don't want. She said she wasn't sure how it worked, but there seemed to be some mysterious connection there, and we can influence what might happen in our lives if we watch how we're thinking. I sometimes like to think of doubt as part of a dark force in life and faith as the force of light.

Some doubt is normal, but I will try to spend most of the day "in the light" by surrounding myself with people who help me believe in myself.

July

Happiness is a choice
that can be made dozens of times daily.

You might think your happiness depends on others, but it doesn't. Let's say your dad yells at you for being on the phone when he was trying to call home. His anger doesn't have to make you unhappy unless you take his words and dwell on them. You could, instead, agree that he is right and give him a hug. You can take any situation and turn it around.

I've seen stories on television about tragedies. I used to wonder how people could be happy despite the tragedy, but I understand now. Whatever we dwell on influences our happiness. Things will happen that will cause us to feel sad or angry. It's good to talk about these feelings and honor them, but to continue to hang on to them can make life harder than it needs to be.

I can choose when to express feelings and when to let them go.

July 2

God is the friend of silence.

Mother Teresa

My parents are always telling me that it's important to be alone sometimes and enjoy it. I would almost always rather be with friends or be busy doing something. But the other day I spent the afternoon alone, reading my book. I felt so peaceful. I have noticed that when I play the piano or get my markers out and draw, I feel calm. Perhaps it is when I am alone and quiet that the spiritual part of me comes out. This part of me helps me feel peaceful and more sure of myself in a quiet way.

Quiet time is time that fills my spirit. I know that this is an important part of me.

Remember to share.

I recently read a book about a girl named Charlotte who couldn't keep a friend for long. This bewildered her. She invited boys and girls to her house for parties. She had stacks of neat games, videos, and CDs, and all the soda and snacks you would want. But she got no invitations back. Her dad asked her one simple question: "Do you ever let your friends make up the rules?"

Everyone who has read the book knows Charlotte's answer. She said, "Well, at my house, I get to make the rules." Her dad said that was her problem. Do you often feel like you should get to be in charge at your house? Taking turns with our friends and being kind rather than bossy is what it takes to make and keep friends. My dad is always saying, "She's your guest. Let her choose first or be served first." Even when he isn't home, I try to remember this.

I may want to make the rules today, but I also want friends. I know what I need to do.

July 4

Responsible behavior is expected of us.

Admitting when we have been wrong or not kind is a sign of maturity. But we generally don't assume responsibility for our actions until we have no alternative. It's far easier to blame someone. We learn to blame while we are children by seeing others doing that. But following a poor example is no excuse when we get older. To be willing to stand up and say, "I did it," when you've been inconsiderate is worthy of imitation.

Taking responsibility for our actions may seem a bit overwhelming at first. Old habits are stubborn. Willingness to admit that a change is necessary is the first step. The next step is to practice watching exactly what our actions are. That way we can consciously choose a better response to a similar circumstance in the future. Can you come up with one example of how you might have acted differently in the past few days, in a way that you would feel better about deep inside?

I may not want to claim responsibility for all that I do and say today, but that's what I need to do. I will try my best.

Sometimes imagining outcomes helps us make a decision.

Last week I planned a sleepover at my house. My stepmother said I could invite three girls. I worried about who to pick because Jill, my best friend, doesn't like Annette, and Annette had invited me to her house recently. It seemed like I should invite her for sure. Melissa said she could come but only if she brought her cousin, who was going to be visiting for the weekend. What a mess.

My stepmother suggested that I close my eyes and envision how the evening might look. She said whoever came easily to my mind might be the ones to invite. I did this, and guess who I invited? Annette, Melissa, and her cousin. We had a wonderful time. I hope Jill doesn't get mad at me for leaving her out, but I did what seemed best. Have you ever tried to resolve a problem by closing your eyes and letting a picture of how it might look come to mind?

Letting a picture come to my mind is a way of figuring out which decision will feel the best.

July 6

To avoid pain at all costs forces us to reject half the lessons life can teach.

Jan Pishok

Every person has many lessons to learn. My grandfather says that's why we are born. But I wonder how old we must be before our lessons begin. My new baby sister doesn't already have lessons, does she? When I asked Dad about this, he laughed and said Molly could grow a little before she had to start her homework. When I think about my life, I realize I have been assigned many lessons.

Not all lessons happen in school. Learning to listen when someone is talking to me and learning to say please and thank you at every opportunity are lessons for everywhere, not just school. Learning how important each person is to the human race is one of the most important lessons of all.

I wonder if I will recognize each of my lessons today.

Loneliness comes and goes.

My mom and I went to visit my grandmother last night at the nursing home. After she fell and broke her hip, Grandma needed help to get dressed, take a bath, and walk. When her hip heals she'll move back into her apartment. She said it's lonely in the nursing home. She's used to having all her neighbors in for coffee.

Are you ever lonely? When Abby went to her dad's house for the summer, I was lonely. I was used to seeing her every day. I pray she doesn't go there this year. My dad said that having a hobby can relieve loneliness. Having friends is wonderful, but we need to be able to entertain ourselves, too. He got into photography as a hobby. It was a way of making some new friends. He met John at a photography class and now they play golf together.

If I feel lonely today, I might try writing a story, drawing, or playing some music.

July 8

Being thin is important to lots of girls,
but what's more important
is being considerate and intelligent.

I've noticed that some of my skirts are too tight this year. Of course I'm growing, but I don't want to be chubby. Everyone at school makes fun of Teri because she is fat. Mom says Teri has a health problem and the medication is what has made her fat. It's cruel of kids to make fun of her. Mom says it's too bad that models are so thin. The rest of us feel fat in comparison, even though we're just fine. I agree, but I still don't want to be overweight, even a little bit.

My mom says I can do a lot to control how much I weigh, because what we eat affects how big we get. I could eat more vegetables and fruit and less pizza. Not always though! Mom says bone structure has a lot to do with our size, too. I'm tall for my age. I will naturally be a bigger girl than Abby will ever be. That's OK, I guess.

I will feel good about how I look if I mainly eat foods that are good for me.

It makes you feel virtuous when you forgive people.
L. M. Montgomery

I am mad at Veronica. She told all my friends about the trouble I got into with my dad. I was embarrassed, especially when some of the girls laughed. What embarrassed me so much is that my dad swore at me, in front of her, and she didn't keep it a secret like she promised to. Mom agreed that Veronica should have kept her promise, but we all make mistakes. I told Veronica I was angry and disappointed, and she apologized. Mom says I should let it go now.

I need to think about this. To get over being mad means I have to forgive Veronica. I'm not sure I want to. Mom reminded me that she has to forgive me almost every day for forgetting something she's asked me to do. For example, she wants me to call home when I'm going to be more than fifteen minutes late, and I almost never remember.

Other people have to forgive me quite often.
I will practice forgiving others today.

July 10

Uncertainty about how your life will turn out keeps it interesting. Right?

We can't be certain of so many things. Can you be certain that your best friend won't ever move away? That happened to me. Susie and I had been in the same room since preschool, and last year her family moved to Detroit because her mom got a big promotion. We had talked about being friends even when we got to college. She doesn't come back here for visits because her grandmother moved with them.

My dad says that living with uncertainty and change is good for us even if we don't like it. He says it taught him to ask God for understanding when things changed that he hadn't counted on. Last year he suddenly lost his job because the company he worked for went bankrupt. He had thought he would work there until he retired. Because he was used to asking God for help, he was able to handle the change. Getting another job took time, though.

We cannot be certain of how things will go today. I will try to enjoy this uncertainty and open my heart to all the day's possibilities.

Generosity warms the giver and the receiver.

There are many ways to be generous. Giving money counts as one way. My grandfather says it's good to give away one dime for every dollar you earn. He gives his money to organizations that help poor people. He suggested I consider doing this with my allowance. I've been thinking about it, but I haven't done it yet. Would you consider doing something like that?

My mother says we can be generous with our time. For instance, helping someone who's stuck in the snow or raking leaves for an elderly neighbor, just as a gesture of kindness, is being generous. Taking the time to listen to others who have problems is an example of generosity, too. Giving someone undivided attention shows a generous spirit.

Are you as generous as you might be? Did you realize there were so many ways to show your generosity?

I can take the time to warm my world and someone else's in many ways.

July 12

I know that you cannot hate other people without hating yourself.

Oprah Winfrey

Have you ever said you hated someone? My stomach actually hurts when I'm full of hate, like I have knots inside. Carol, my sister, says that hatred can make a person sick. Our neighbor ends up in the hospital often. Carol says it's because he is so mean and hates everyone.

My reaction to such a mean person is to want to get back at them. But that just keeps the conflict going, and my stomach continues to hurt. Being so full of hate never solves anything. It hurts everybody. It's hard to give up my feelings of hate, but I sure am tired of stomachaches.

I have many good feelings to choose from today. I'll choose one now.

There is always an open door
on the other side of anger.

Hanging on to anger and resentment keeps us from growing and changing in the ways that are important. When a person is resentful, she's letting something that happened in the past take charge of how she's feeling right this minute. For instance, yesterday my mom was at the grocery store in the express line. She hadn't counted what she had in her cart, and she had twelve things, rather than ten, like the sign says. The woman behind her complained to Mom about not following directions. Mom ignored her, but she was so angry that she drove too fast coming home and got a ticket for speeding.

At dinner she explained how her anger and resentment had complicated her entire day. She could have let the whole thing go, apologized to the woman for not counting her groceries, and felt OK when she left the store. Instead, she drove too fast, and it cost her almost a hundred dollars. Our resentments are good opportunities for us to look at how we might have behaved differently.

It's always possible to find a way to move through any anger or resentment I feel.

July 14

Worrying can become our constant companion.

Worrying can become a habit, and my dad says we always worry about the wrong things. He worried that he wouldn't get through college. Of course, the worry made him study extra hard. He finally graduated last year. We were so proud of him. He went to college part time for twelve years!

Sometimes we worry about dumb stuff, like whether a certain person will notice a new outfit, but boys never pay attention to those things. My mom worries about her hair not looking perfect whenever she gets her picture taken. I think her hair looks the same all the time.

I worry about not being one of the popular girls in our class. My grandmother says this was a worry she had when she was in high school. She said that she handled it by just trying to be a good friend to a few people, and never gossiping behind anyone's back. She said it worked.

Too many people worry too much. I want to worry less.

We can't take any credit for our talents.
It's how we use them that counts.

Madeleine L'Engle

Every person is blessed with a particular talent. You might not believe this. I thought my stepmother was just trying to make me feel better because I didn't get chosen to be in our class play. She suggested that I volunteer to help paint the scenes. Guess what I discovered? I'm good at skctching large pictures. Everyone was surprised at how realistic the background looked. The trees looked as though they were swaying in the breeze.

If I hadn't been passed over for a part in the play, I would never have discovered one of my talents. So if you haven't figured out where your talents lie, just be patient. When you least expect it, it will become known to you. Helena, my stepmother, said she discovered her ability to write quite by accident, too. She has written three books and they've all been published.

I'm glad I've discovered one talent. I will be on the lookout for others today.

July 16

There are people who . . . accept whatever happens day to day without struggle or question or regret.

Celeste De Blasis

"There are many things that happen in life that you simply have to accept." My dad was lecturing us this morning at the breakfast table. My brother and I didn't want to help clean up the kitchen before joining our friends outside. He wouldn't give in. Accepting that we have chores and that they always come before play is a rule in our house. Are you expected to do chores?

Dad says he has to accept things all the time that he isn't happy about. He didn't get the job he had applied for, so he didn't ask for a loan for a new car. He was disappointed. Acceptance isn't easy even for adults. He said that one of his favorite prayers is the one about asking for the serenity to accept what he cannot change and the courage to change the things he can.

I will remember to pray for serenity when I need to accept something hard.

Celebrate your life and hear your spirit sing.

Elizabeth L.

Have you thought about gratitude recently? It's not a word that I use often, but my father says we need to make it part of our conscious thought every day. It's his feeling that the frequent expression of gratitude could change the entire world. Here is how it would work, at least according to my dad.

His theory is that if more people were grateful for what they have, then there would be far less greed. Greed is when having things is more important than caring for people. And I've noticed that when gratitude is in my heart, I love so much about my life. Sometimes I just have to remind myself of all that I am grateful for.

Gratitude helps me to stop and be glad for all that I have.

July 18

Faith is believing that everything will work out.

My Sunday school teacher is always talking to our class about "developing faith." He says you develop it like you develop any skill. You practice. He told us a story about how he developed a good golf swing. He stood in front of his closet mirror every morning and watched himself swing a club. He did this at least twenty-five times a day. Within a month, he was hitting the ball much farther. To have faith, it helps to practice having it every time you get the chance—even as many as twenty-five times a day.

This may sound silly, but I've been practicing his method, and I'm feeling happier most of the time. My aunt Sylvia believes that having faith means letting God be in charge. It means knowing you will be OK no matter what happens.

I will practice having faith every chance I get.

July 19

Forgiveness is an exercise that needs practice.

What does it mean to forgive? This concept confused me when I was younger. I had heard the word and I had read it many times, but I didn't really get what it meant. Now I understand forgiveness, but there are some words in my vocabulary that I use but don't understand all that well. I know how to pronounce them and can even use them in a sentence, but I'm puzzled about their exact meaning.

Something that happened in my family when I was in the sixth grade made forgiveness clear to me. My dad packed a suitcase and left when we were all away, and didn't explain anything. My mom was so sad. My little sister cried. My grandmother was furious, and I was confused and scared. I had seen my parents hugging the day before Dad disappeared. Then about three days later, he came back. He told us that he had gotten fired and was so ashamed, he didn't want to face any of us. My mom put her arms around him and said, "I understand and I forgive you for leaving." He cried. The rest of us cried, too. Forgiveness can be powerful. Wouldn't you agree?

I will be ready to forgive someone today.

July 20

Laughter we can never overrate.

May Sarton

My grandfather has the neatest laugh. He's fat, so when he laughs, he shakes all over. That makes me laugh. When I'm around him, I laugh a lot. Sometimes just thinking about him makes me laugh, especially when I remember the time he laughed so hard that he tipped over our canoe. We were laughing hysterically by then but somehow managed to get back in the boat.

In science class last year, Miss Bowen told us about a person who used laughter to help cure himself of a terrible disease. He used laughter in the same way you would use medicine. He watched movies that made him laugh hard. The laughter, he's convinced, somehow healed him. This makes me think that there are more reasons for laughing than for not.

I love to laugh. I will let laughter come easily today.

When fear seizes, change what you are doing.
Jean George

My grandmother said that she always talked to her favorite doll when she was a girl and felt afraid. That made her feel less anxious. I thought that seemed silly, but I often go into my bedroom and lie on my bed, close my eyes, and talk quietly to myself. That's probably not any different. My friend Lindsay says she doesn't talk, but she writes in her journal. Mother says the important thing is to have some action you can take when you're afraid. The action gets you moving beyond the fear.

My mom's fears go away when she chats with God. She considers God a friend who wants to help her be free of her fears. Mom says God is always listening even when I think I'm only talking to myself.

Fear doesn't stick around long unless you keep it tight in your mind. When you put something else there, like an image of God or a kind friend, the fear blows away like smoke.

Instead of holding on to my fear, I will give it away.

July 22

Random acts of kindness brighten our world.

Making the decision to be kind makes how a person lives so much easier. I didn't believe this before, but lately I've been watching how my kindness changes the people around me. Offering to help my dad pick up the trash in the alley by our house brought a big smile to his face. After we were done, he suggested we go for a treat. I got my favorite: a hot fudge sundae.

After I helped Mr. Silverstein gather the walnuts from his yard, his wife brought us a batch of homemade candy with walnuts in it. Last week my older sister offered to check my math assignment for errors. I didn't even ask for the help, and her kindness paid off big time. She found three mistakes. I would have gotten a B rather than an A on it. Kindness always pays off in some way.

I will count all the ways I am kind today and pay attention to the kindness I receive.

We can't always be sure what the outcome of a sad circumstance will be.

I love my grandmother. She is retired, but she used to teach high school English. When she'd come to stay with us, she would bring wonderful books to read to my sister and me. Sometimes she brought stories that her students had written. I'll never forget one that was so sad I cried, but I ended up happy before the end.

The story was about a disabled girl, Lisa, who had a dog as her companion. She went nowhere alone. Misty, the dog, was always by her side. One day they walked to a park. Some older boys started throwing rocks at Misty, and one hit him in the eye. Because he was supposed to protect Lisa, he didn't chase after the boys. An older woman saw his eye bleeding and came to help. She walked Misty and Lisa home. Misty went blind in that eye and had to give up being Lisa's protector. The woman became a friend to the family and gave them her own dog to work as a protector for Lisa. Although his work was over, Misty stayed as the family's pet.

If I think something is sure to have a bad ending, I will be patient. I may be wrong.

July 24

Listening is more than just being quiet.

Listening is one of the most respectful actions we can take, but it is not always easy to listen when someone is talking to you. My aunt Karen's voice is loud, and I have a hard time listening to her. Often I wish I could cover my ears. Hayley's grandfather talks so softly that I can hardly hear him, no matter how hard I try to listen. But the important thing about listening is that it honors other people when you listen. Do you understand the importance of honoring others? My stepmother said that listening shows the other person that nothing is more important than he or she in that moment. We all need to feel important, she says.

I don't like it when I'm trying to tell my dad something and he keeps reading the paper. Last night I was talking to Teri on the phone and she started talking to her brother right in the middle of my sentence. I was hurt because I was telling her a secret. Since I know how it feels not to be listened to, I will try harder to honor others by listening.

I will be a good listener today.

Everyone has value.

I worry sometimes that I'm not very important. Mother says this is something everybody worries about occasionally, even adults. She reminded me that we are all important, even the smallest baby and the oldest human being.

I hope I can remember that. Sometimes I ignore certain people at school because I don't think they're so important. Maybe I can look at them more carefully. Perhaps I haven't noticed their good points. Mother says that seeing the good in others brings out our own good.

Today I will look for at least one good point in someone I usually don't pay attention to.

July 26

Arguments never feel good.

When I don't get enough sleep, I get irritable and often start arguments before I even realize it. Mom says it's immaturity. Disagreements don't have to end up becoming mean-spirited arguments. She says that mature people agree to disagree.

I know that arguing never solves anything. I end up having an uncomfortable feeling in my stomach and hiding out in my bedroom, missing out on all the action at the teen center. I avoid that place especially if I've had an argument with a friend. Arguing never gives me more friends. It has even cost me a few.

I will make a different choice today if I think I'm about to get into an argument.

Changing your mind can be easier than you think.

Do you realize you can change how you feel simply by changing your mind about something that has happened? I doubted this, but that was because I heard it from my mom's new friend, Phillip, and I'm not sure I like him. I tried doing what he said, though.

The first time I tried it, I was sad because I hadn't been invited to go with the neighbors to a drive-in movie. I pouted for a while, then went into my bedroom and picked up a book I hadn't read for a long time. It was about a girl who moved away in the middle of the ninth grade. She was sad, but her new classmates convinced her that they liked her. Right away she was invited to join the girl's basketball team. She realized that everything always works out.

I felt OK after rereading this story. It was not a big deal that Whitcombs hadn't invited me to go with them. Being alone and reading a good book can help me feel better. That's what I've heard my mom say many times.

Time alone can feel satisfying even when it isn't my first choice.

July 28

Coincidences are really plans
God hasn't told us about.

Sandra L.

Did you know that some people believe there is no such thing as a coincidence? My grandfather says that everything that happens is absolutely supposed to happen. Whatever happens is never accidental, or coincidental, according to his philosophy.

I was sad when my friend Katie transferred to another school. But when I saw her again at a ballet class, she told me about a friend she'd made at her new school. It turned out to be April, who'd been by best friend until third grade! I've missed her often since she moved away. Now when I visit Katie, I get to see April sometimes, too.

Often changes work out better than we expect them to.

Friendship is a gift we are lucky to receive.

Ruth C.

Hillary and I used to leave Rachel out of our fun. She was the newest girl in our class last year, and she treated most of us as though we were from some other planet. She exchanged nothing but dirty looks and rude comments with most of the girls. She ignored the boys completely. Mr. Cruz had a talk with her, but it didn't change her behavior.

Hillary's mom said that perhaps Rachel was scared about moving to a new city and a new school and her fear made her behave that way. When I'm afraid, I'm really quiet, not threatening and unkind. Hillary's mom suggested we ignore Rachel's behavior and invite her to join us at lunch. Rachel ate with us, and she thanked us for asking her. She even said she was afraid no one liked her and she had begged her mom to move back to Saint Louis. We're glad that didn't happen. She's becoming our friend.

Sometimes a crusty outer shell hides a sensitive soul inside.

July 30

Easy does it.

I get nervous about a lot of things. Every time we have a pop quiz in history class, I get sick to my stomach. I generally do OK, but I always worry. And I can't stand waiting for my boyfriend to call to ask me to the movies on the weekend. When I focus on having fun with my friends and not waiting for him, I'm happier.

Mom says she tells herself "Easy does it" to stop feeling uptight. She says you take a deep breath and let go of whatever idea is troubling you. The idea may come back, but you breathe again and let it go. Taking all the experiences in your life more easily isn't all that hard with practice. She even has an "Easy does it" bumper sticker on her car.

Maybe I should put an "Easy does it" bumper sticker on my dresser mirror. I would like to drop some of my worry time.

Listening to your thoughts might surprise you.

Does it ever occur to you to do a favor for a friend who isn't expecting it? My friend Jody surprised me by offering to help me rake our yard. Dad had made me come home from her house because I hadn't finished the job. I hate to rake, and I would never have offered to help her. But she stayed until we were finished. It took only half the time it would have taken me, and I got only half the blisters.

I asked her why she offered, and she said the idea just popped into her head, so she thought she would say it out loud. Ideas come to me, but I don't often follow through with them. I thought about writing a letter to my grandfather yesterday, but didn't do it. He has been in the hospital for a few weeks. He would have been happy to get a letter from me. My mom says good ideas are coming to us for good reasons, and if more people acted on the ideas for being kind that came to them, we would be living in a happier world.

I will follow through on the good and kind ideas that come into my mind today.

August

People need joy quite as much as clothing.
Margaret Collier Graham

"Joy" is a tiny word. But with the help of my parents, I have learned it can fill my life in a big way. Joy can result from good health. It can come from a hobby that is fun. Mine is sketching birds. Mom said she was filled with joy when I learned to walk and talk. She even feels joy making a pizza for dinner or taking a skiing trip with her friends.

The easy part of joy is that if you think about your life even a little, you will see many reasons to be filled with joy. You get joy from many experiences. But what if some experiences are sad? Feeling joyful hasn't seemed possible at times, like when my grandmother died. Mom helped all of us remember how much fun Grandma had every time she stayed at our house. That put a smile on my face, especially when I looked at the picture Dad took of her in my bed with all my stuffed animals.

My world has many moments of joy.

August 2

Believing in God is an individual thing.

Not everyone believes in God. I was surprised when I went to Samantha's house and heard her dad say something mean about the Bible. We don't read from the Bible often, but we do talk about the way God can help us, and we have a Bible on the bookshelf. When Samantha and I were alone in her bedroom, I asked her if she believed in God and she seemed embarrassed. She said they never talk about it because her dad says God doesn't exist. I was shocked.

I worried about this because I thought Mom wouldn't want me to go to Samantha's house anymore, and that would have been devastating. Samantha and I are writing a play together. Mom said that everyone has a right to believe whatever they want. Living in a democracy, like we have in the United States, gives us the right to believe whatever we want to. I'm relieved. But I'm a bit worried, too. If Samantha doesn't believe in God, what will happen to her when she dies?

Mom says I don't need to worry about Samantha's beliefs. I need to just concentrate on my own.

If we are patient, we usually will eventually understand why something turned out the way it did.

Everything happens for a reason. For instance, when it rains, even if I am in the middle of a ball game, I understand from science class that atmospheric conditions are what causes rain. When I trip over the stool in the family room and skin my knee, it is because I am not watching where I am walking. My carelessness is at fault.

However, the reasons for some consequences are not so obvious at first. Mr. Sidney, our neighbor, is ill. His wife told my mom that the doctor said he had to change many of his habits if he wanted to get well. He eats too many fattening foods, drinks too much liquor, never exercises, and smokes cigarettes. There are reasons for his illness, even though you have to look for them.

My grandfather lost his job. That was hard for him to accept at first because he loved his job. What he didn't know was that a better job was waiting for him only a block from his house.

I wonder what will surprise me today.

August 4

Striving for excellence motivates you;
striving for perfection is demoralizing.
Harriet Braiker

I make a lot of mistakes. Some are silly. Some are ludicrous. One that I made last week was the most ludicrous of all, so far. I hurried home after school to get to the craft store before it closed. I dropped my books on the kitchen table, wrote my mom a note, and jumped on my bike. I got to the store, bought the thread I needed, and rode home. I took the back way home because the traffic was heavy. I was home before I realized I had the wrong bike. When I called the shop to tell them, they were closed. I didn't have any idea whose bike I had.

Over dinner, we talked about my dilemma. Dad said that the owner of the bike I had probably rode my bike home. He was wrong. When I went to the shop the next day, my bike was still there. I had not even locked it. I was lucky no one stole it. The woman who owns the store said she didn't know whose bike I had, but she would keep it until the owner claimed it. I guess that person makes mistakes, too. She never even came back for her bike.

I can't be perfect, but I can avoid a lot of mistakes today if I slow down.

Asking for help makes two people feel connected and important.

Jo Reed

How do you feel about asking your teachers for extra help in a subject that is hard for you? Lots of kids get help in algebra in Mr. Dixon's classroom after school. Ms. Katz is always telling our class she'll help us write our autobiographies if we need it. But for some reason, I hate to admit I need help. This doesn't seem to bother Elise or Veronica, my two best friends. They often stay after school for extra help. I wonder why it bothers me.

Mom says I probably got this trait naturally. Neither she nor my dad used to admit they needed help. They both thought that it was best to figure everything out alone. Guess where they got their traits?

Asking for help is good, Mom has learned. She says it strengthens you, even though it seems like the opposite would be true. She hopes I can learn this more quickly than she did. Dad has yet to learn it.

I will try to ask for help if I need it today. I want the confidence it can give me.

August 6

> *I was an excellent student until ten,*
> *and then my mind began to wander.*
>
> Grace Paley

Is your mind a good friend to you? Does it take direction from your heart? It's true that all sorts of things seem to come into a person's mind. My little sister wrote all over her bedroom wall with a pink crayon and then she told Dad that a voice in her mind told her to do it. He laughed hard—when she wasn't around to hear him.

Many times I find myself dwelling on things that seem crazy. Like, I'll imagine I'm in another family, living a different life. Mom says I have a vivid imagination, which could be to my advantage when I'm older. Maybe I'll be a writer someday and write science fiction or mystery books. But my mind makes me afraid, too. It tells me I can't achieve the goals I've set for myself. I have to listen more to my heart when this happens. It knows what a capable girl I am.

I will cherish my heart thoughts today.

Getting left out feels awful.

When was the last time your friends got together but didn't invite you? If you're lucky, this has never happened to you. I've been disappointed like this many times. Mom says I shouldn't take it personally; most likely my friends didn't intend to leave me out. Everyone thinks everyone else has been called and doesn't realize one person was missed. The last time it happened, Denise, Beth, and Lisa all called to apologize. I felt better.

I've had to leave friends out, too. When my grandmother gave me three tickets to see *Cinderella* at the children's theater, I couldn't ask all three girls. I had to choose two, and it wasn't easy. I put all of their names in a hat and pulled out two. That way, no one got their feelings hurt.

Getting left out hurts, but it happens to all of us.

August 8

Offering friendship to a new student helps both people.

There are thirty-two kids in my homeroom. I know them all, but I'm not good friends with each of them. We had a discussion about friendship last week. We had to write an essay on what it meant to be a good friend. Mr. Whitmore asked for volunteers to read their essays. Naturally, Cynthia raised her hand. She is such a teacher's pet. Her essay was incredibly good, though. She has an excellent vocabulary. She uses words I'm not familiar with, but I don't want her to know that.

What she said was that extending your hand in friendship to someone new was like receiving a gift you hadn't expected. You have something to offer to each person you meet, and everyone you meet has something to offer to you and everyone he or she meets. You won't ever know what you're missing unless you make the first move. The class agreed her essay was the best and was good advice. What it taught me was that my homeroom is full of "gifts" I have not yet opened.

I will be open to the gifts inside people around me.

Showing you care can change a person's life.

There are as many ways of showing you care as there are people in this universe. Think about all the ways your parents have shown you that they care. You have a home. You've learned to read, which means they've made sure you're getting an education. You have clothing and food. And what about the allowance you earn?

Now think about the ways that teachers show they care. They might go over the same problems in math, again and again, until everyone understands. They might stay after class when necessary. Ms. Richardson went out of her way to introduce a new student to us at lunch. I'm sure this helped Rebecca feel at home.

Showing you care can be a simple act. Even smiling at a person whose name you don't know shows that you care. So does holding the door for an elderly person when you're rushing into the grocery store.

I can show more than one person I care today.

August 10

Those who are unhappy
have no need for anything in this world
but people capable of giving them their attention.

Simone Weil

Wanting some attention is normal. Everybody wants to be listened to. How you get the attention is another matter, though. Sometimes kids whine or get in trouble just to get attention.

What I have learned, from my older sister, is that if I want attention, I can ask for it. She said she would stop what she was doing if I needed to talk with her, and that most people would do that. The problem is that few of us realize how simple it is to get attention. Our embarrassment about needing it prevents us from seeking it in a healthy way.

Whenever I need to, I can ask a special someone to listen or pay attention to me.

No whining allowed!

A girl in my class is always whining. She whines about getting called on when she's forgotten her homework. She whines when she goes through the cafeteria line because she hates the food most days. She whines because not many people ask her to parties.

Whining is a sign of self-pity. It's pretty easy to get trapped in self-pity. I have done it a zillion times. But I know that you can change that feeling with a little effort. The way that works best for me is to make a list of all the things that are good in my life. At the top of the list is my boyfriend. Next is the fact that I'm pretty smart in most subjects. Mom suggested I be grateful for my excellent health. Her younger sister had polio and never got to have a normal childhood.

Nothing in my life will be improved by whining.
If I forget that today, I will start a new list.

August 12

Prayer is a private activity.

I overheard my grandmother praying last night. It made me feel safe because she was asking God to watch over me whenever I'm out after dark. We live in a wooded area so that's a good prayer.

I didn't mean to listen, but she doesn't realize she's talking as loud as she often is. She was praying for my mom, too. She's lost her job again, and Grandma asked God to help her find the right one. I wish God would help her quit drinking. That's why she keeps losing her job.

Do you pray? When I was younger, I used to say the prayer, "Now I lay me down to sleep." Probably every kid knows it, but when I got older, it seemed silly to me. Now I don't have a regular prayer, and sometimes I think it would comfort me to have one.

There are many ways to pray. I just need to find one that works for me.

Anger doesn't have to rule our behavior.

Anger is simply an emotion. I was reading a great book the other night about a family similar to mine. The dad lost his temper easily, a lot like my stepdad. When the mom in the story talked to him about this, he kept saying, "Anger is simply an emotion. It is neither bad nor good." That was like discussions my parents have had.

What do you think about anger? Do your parents have an opinion about it? My dilemma is that if something happens that causes me to want to yell, I don't know what to do other than yell. My mother has been to counselors, and she says that counselors tell you to try admitting to someone that you are angry and then you might feel less like yelling or stomping around. Maybe I will try this.

If I start to feel angry today, I will quietly tell someone.

August 14

Responsibilities accompany our growth.

I have a lot more responsibility around the house than I did when I was younger. Because I'm the oldest girl in our family, I get a lot of jobs dumped on me. At least, that's what it feels like. I'm the only one strong enough to haul the trash out. I'm the only one Mom trusts to put the dishes in the dishwasher. I detest that job, but Mom gives me no sympathy because she had to do the dishes by hand when she was a kid. She had six brothers and sisters, all younger.

I'm trying a more positive way of looking at responsibility. It shows that I'm maturing, which means having more freedom. For instance, I'm allowed to go to movies alone or with friends. I can spend my allowance on whatever I want. I get to watch television in my room until ten o'clock. Maybe having certain responsibilities isn't all that bad.

I will try to appreciate my responsibilities today. They are signs that I'm growing up.

Most people feel shy sometimes.

I feel shy in certain situations. Other times I don't feel shy at all. My best friend, Miranda, says she is always shy except when we're together. Feeling shy can be a hard personality trait to have because it can keep you from enjoying opportunities. But it can keep you out of trouble, too. I was too shy to follow the new girl in our class when she went into the restroom after school. She got caught smoking. What a relief that I wasn't with her.

Last week, I was invited to go to a party at Joseph's house. He is the new guy in my science class. I was afraid to say yes right away because I didn't know who else had been invited. Miranda was not asked. Neither was Rebecca. When I got home from school, I asked Mom what to do. She encouraged me to take a risk and go. She said that unexpected invitations are often the best ones. That was how she met Dad. Now I'm excited about going to the party.

Shyness is human. I don't have to let it stop me from doing what I want to do.

August 16

We all have limitations, but they need not stop us.

Does your size limit you in some of the activities you pursue? I have much shorter legs than most girls on my softball team, which means I can't outrun most players. I've practiced running, but my legs just can't go any faster. The coach says we all have limitations. Mine is just more obvious in sports.

I often feel that the other girls wish I would drop off the team. Someone quicker would mean more wins. Dad says I shouldn't worry about this. Winning isn't the most important thing. The coach agrees. She says that having a good time and being a good sport about winning or losing are more important to her. I love playing the game and being part of the team. The coach, my dad, and I feel my attitude is a valuable contribution.

Dad says I should focus more on my strengths than my limitations.

Discontentment need not last forever.

In school yesterday, I was preoccupied with the way Wendy was acting. We were best friends for five years. Now she seldom includes me in anything. She acknowledges my presence, but she doesn't act like she remembers we were best friends. My stepmom said her best friend in high school quit speaking to her in their senior year and she never got an explanation. It isn't easy to concentrate on schoolwork when something like this is going on in your life.

What do you do when you are preoccupied with a problem? Maybe your problem isn't like mine, but do you have a solution you rely on? When my stepmom and I talked, she said that when she's worried about something, she makes a list of all the good things in her life. This keeps her from dwelling on what's bothering her. Problems seem smaller when you do this.

I will have paper and a pen handy today if I begin to dwell on a problem.

August 18

Inspiration often grows out of what we admire.

Do you know what it's like to feel inspired? I heard my older brother say he felt inspired to write a story. I heard Mom say that Abraham Lincoln inspired her to try to do her best when she was a girl. I looked up the word on my computer and found a lot of examples of what the word can mean. I realized I had been inspired lots of times but hadn't realized it. Every time I'm flooded with the feeling of wanting to do something, I'm inspired.

I've been inspired to try to get all A's on my report card. I'm inspired to try out for basketball next year. I'm inspired to keep my room cleaner so that I can ask for an increase in my allowance. That would mean saving money faster for the tennis bracelet I want. I'm frequently inspired. Whoever was inspired to write the dictionary sure helped me.

I wonder what I will be inspired to do today?

My experiences are colorful threads in the weaving of my life.

We live in a purposeful world. Until my grandfather explained the concept to me, I didn't get it. He said it means that nothing happens without a reason. He believes that even the tragedies that occur in our families have their reason for happening. Every element in a person's entire life is a thread that is helping to weave a big and colorful picture.

I like looking at life this way. It helps me accept some of the troubling and crazy experiences in my life. I used to wonder why I was the last one picked to play ball after school and the first one picked to be on our class spelling team. Now I can see that my strengths and weaknesses play their part in the picture that is me. I can even see how my brother's long hospital stay taught our whole family to appreciate one another more. My grandfather says misfortunes are often our most purposeful experiences.

I will remember that whatever happens today has an important purpose.

August 20

One half of the world cannot understand the pleasures of the other.

Jane Austen

Are you and your brothers and sisters alike? Even twins are different. Rhonda and Reba, girls who were in my class last year while I still lived in New Jersey, looked nothing alike, and Rhonda was much friendlier. My brother and I are very different, according to Grandma. He is bossy, but comical. She told me in private that I was much more polite.

My grandma said that if you paid close attention, you would observe differences everywhere. No two people really look alike, no two families are alike in all of their beliefs. No two dogs or cats behave alike. It's the differences that make us interesting.

Wouldn't it be boring if every one of your friends looked and behaved like every other friend? You wouldn't even be sure who you were with. And yet, don't we sometimes complain that others should be just like us? Lots of arguments occur over different opinions. But we need all of them, don't we?

Differences are necessary but hard to accept. I will try to appreciate the differences in my friends today.

"One day at a time" is a good slogan for living.

Our refrigerator is covered with sayings and pictures that my mom has cut out of magazines. She even has a couple of bumper stickers on it. Her favorite one is "One day at a time." She explained to us that it helps her remember that all she can deal with is what is happening today, right now. Worrying about what may happen next week or next year keeps her from handling what she needs to take care of now.

I have thought a lot about that bumper sticker. I spend a lot of time dwelling on the future. I wonder who I might date when I turn sixteen. I wonder if I should have long or short hair. I wonder most about the kind of career I might have. And I wonder which of my friends will still live here. Mom says that every time we let our minds wander to the future, we are missing out on something that can never be repeated again. I think a good slogan for a bumper sticker is "Pay attention now!"

I don't want to miss out on anything. That means paying attention to the here and now, today.

August 22

A peacefulness follows any decision.

Rita Mae Brown

We're never too young to improve the way we make decisions. Parents or other adults in our lives make many of the big decisions for us, but we make decisions about how we'll treat our family and friends. Do we listen to other opinions and advice? It's a decision we must make. Do we apply our skills in school? It's a decision. Do we decide to smoke if someone offers us a cigarette? Do we put ourselves down when we make a mistake? Or do we forgive our mistakes like my grandmother would forgive them? These are decisions.

Sometimes I have choices for what to do in a day, and I keep changing my mind about what to do. It's hard to choose one, especially if a couple of the choices sound fun or I feel like I'll disappoint someone or miss something. My mom says I need to take some quiet time and see what feels most right. This has worked for me several times. I feel a peacefulness once I've made the decision that's most right for me.

I will slow down today to make sure that my good decisions stay in charge.

Helping others benefits me in a heartwarming way.

When was the last time you offered to help a classmate with a project that was especially hard? If you can't remember an instance right off, it was too long ago. Mr. Henry says that all the great humanitarians we read about in history had one thing in common: They put others first and were always ready to offer help.

We each picked a person we admired who lived at least fifty years ago and searched the computer or did research in the library for information on them. It gave us a lot of good ideas about the many ways to help other people. I chose Eleanor Roosevelt, the wife of President Franklin Roosevelt. She worked hard for the benefit of African Americans in our country. She cared that they have the same opportunities as she had to live whatever kind of life they wanted.

I will try to follow Eleanor Roosevelt's example and show that I care about others.

August 24

Every relationship is a teacher.
Brenda M. Schaeffer

Most of us have ten or more significant relationships. Parents are usually at the top of the list. Even if you live with just one parent, you might see the other one regularly and maybe some grandparents, too. Most of us have brothers and sisters and best friends. Lots of us have cousins we see often. Our relationships with our teachers are significant, too. Relationships are really important.

How we get along in our relationships can determine our success in many circumstances. If we fight against our parents all the time, we won't get the encouragement we need to succeed. The same principle applies in school. For instance, if Mr. Switzer has reasons to discipline me all the time rather than to compliment or encourage me, I will not become all that I'm capable of becoming, as a student and as a person. But if I respect and am considerate of my parents, teachers, and friends, I'll have stronger and more caring relationships.

I'll keep in mind today how important my relationships are to me.

Negative thoughts tend to hinder our growth.

Fearing I can't do something often keeps me from even trying. Let me explain. Last year, Tiana, a new girl on my block, got skis for Christmas. She invited me to go to the park to try them out. I was too afraid to try them because my older brother broke his leg skiing last year. Tiana invited Sara instead and they had so much fun. I heard them talking about it.

Fear changes a person's life. My grandmother says that fear is almost like a magnet, attracting the things that we dread might happen, and that learning to think positively can help us with everything in life. She said feeling some fear is normal, but we don't have to let it stop us. We can be like the skier at the top of the hill, heart beating fast, saying "I can do this" and then doing it. Or I can try the phrase Grandma taught me to use: "I am in the right place now and God will help me do whatever I need to do."

I can walk through my fear when I believe I can.

August 26

The mind is like a richly woven tapestry.
Carson McCullers

My grandfather, before he died, told me stories as a way of explaining ideas that were difficult. For instance, he said my mind is connected to my heart, something like the way that my legs are connected to my brain. He said we couldn't see the connection, but it was there. When my heart felt warmth toward a friend, my mind might gently suggest that I say something kind.

It's a pleasant idea, thinking of my heart and mind this way. But I was confused over what had happened all those times I said something mean to my friend or my little sister. Grandfather said people don't always listen to their hearts. When we're tired or worried or even hungry, we sometimes let our minds speak without even considering what our heart might be trying to suggest. When I do this, I cause trouble for myself every time.

My mind wants to listen to my heart, and I will help it today.

Keep it simple.

My grandmother's favorite saying is "Keep it simple." I don't know where she learned this, but she says it a lot. She says everybody makes their life harder than it needs to be because they complicate whatever they're doing. They try to do too much or please too many people at one time.

Sometimes I sign up for too many activities, and it gets complicated remembering all the schedules and managing to do everything and still get my homework done. Last Saturday I had plans for part of the day with Jessica, and then Emily called and I was trying to fit it all in. When I start to feel crabby, I know I'm too busy. My mother says she gets crabby, too, when she's too busy. We've decided to help each other say no to new activities when we're busy. "Keep it simple" is our new slogan, just like my grandmother suggested.

I will keep my activities simple today so I can enjoy what I am doing and feel more peaceful.

August 28

I only have to be what I am.

Roberta Dircks

Do you ever wonder who you are? This may seem silly, but looking in the mirror only shows me how I look on the outside. My grandmother says that who we are is inside of us and can't be seen in the mirror. She said that watching me talk to my friends tells her a lot about who I am on the inside. For example, she said that when I offered to help Julie find her favorite necklace, even though I was considering going to a movie with my dad, it revealed how important Julie's feelings were to me. She said my sensitivity to others was a good inner trait.

Another example she gave me that showed who I am was when I yelled at my little brother for spilling his milk. She said humans are complicated beings. We have good and not-so-good traits. She said the good news is that we can practice the good ones as often as possible and we will have less time to show the other ones.

Who I am today depends on which trait I decide to practice.

If I get thrown off balance,
there are ways to regain my balance.

Let's say you're getting ready for school one morning and you can't find the earrings that match your sweater. The next thing you know, your mom is mad because your breakfast is getting cold and the bus is coming. Maybe you feel off the rest of the day. Some days are like that.

I wish I could remember all the simple suggestions I read in a magazine article last month. The tips were on how a person could prevent a slightly troubled day from becoming a disastrous one. One was to close your eyes, take a few deep breaths, and do whatever the next right thing seems to be. Taking a moment to get quiet within yourself is supposed to alleviate the panic. I tried this and it works. It's like I've been thrown off track, but with some quiet time I can get back on track.

If my day looks like it's headed in the wrong direction,
I will slow down.

August 30

There is hope for all of us.

Mary Beckett

What does hope mean to you? Sandra, my Sunday school teacher, said having hope is a direct path to a more successful life. I asked her if she meant that if you hoped for a better boyfriend, you would get him. Or if you hoped you were taller, you'd suddenly grow. Everybody, even Sandra, laughed. Sandra said hope is a state of mind. She contrasted it with having fear as your state of mind. Someone who is always afraid never accomplishes much because the fear keeps them from trying new activities. If your mind is filled with hope, it's easier to try something new.

Having hope keeps you open to wonderful new ideas and experiences. It's like you have opened the door in your mind so that fresh breezes can blow through. Seeing my mind as having an open door excites me.

Many things are possible in my life if I have hope.

Old habits are strong.

Dorothea Brande

Good habits can be developed and destructive habits can be broken. That's good news, isn't it? Let's say you want to quit biting your nails. This is one of my bad habits. What I try to do is pay closer attention to every move I make. If I watch myself, I can anticipate when I am about to bring my hand toward my mouth. Then I can make a deliberate decision to stop. If I praise myself for not giving in to the habit, that will help too. Praise always helps, no matter where it comes from.

Let's say you want to develop a new positive habit, like always looking directly at the person who is speaking to you. This may sound dumb. You may think you automatically do this, but you don't. For just this one day, pay attention to how many times you're looking somewhere else when your mom says something to you. You'll be surprised at how little you make eye contact when she's speaking. And she's just one person. Pay attention to all the others who speak to you. You might be surprised at how seldom you look directly at the speaker. Yet looking someone in the eyes is an important way to connect with them.

I want more good habits than bad ones. Today is a good day to practice.

September

Change is part of the flow of life.

Nothing stays the same. The clothes you wore last year no longer fit. They might even be out of style. If you didn't ever get a haircut, you eventually would be sitting on your hair. Moving from sixth grade to seventh meant a lot of changes. We move from room to room for our classes. When we were younger, the teachers kept us in one room because they probably figured we'd get lost.

Some changes are more serious. Mandy's parents got divorced. That meant big changes for her family. Mandy misses her dad. He doesn't come around often. When my grandmother got sick, my mother went to stay with her, which meant a lot more work for me at home. I discovered that my dad is a perfectionist. Boy, did he check my work. No phone calls until he was satisfied. I didn't like that change. I try to remember that change is like a river that can't be held back.

I will step into the waters of change with an open heart, to see what I can learn about myself and the others around me.

September 2

To help another is helping yourself as well.

Paige Reed

It's easy to make the decision to be helpful. Once you make it, being helpful can become second nature. Let's say you notice that your neighbor is looking for her newspaper. She is stooped, peering under the bushes. Because she's old, this isn't easy for her. You go to help her without even considering whether you want to. Having made the decision to be helpful whenever you can prompts you to act immediately.

Deciding to be helpful can simplify and enrich our lives. It alleviates the need to ponder what the best response to a situation is. My parents say that "helpfulness is next to godliness." I'm not sure what that means, but I know it's good by the way they say it. If I remember to be helpful when an opportunity arises, I will please at least four people: the person I helped, me, and my parents.

I will look for ways to be helpful today.

Sharing feelings shares the burden.

My stepfather told my sister and me that happiness can be contagious, especially when you share it with someone else. He also said sadness can be lessened by talking with someone about what has made you sad. He believes that letting others know our deepest feelings gives us relief from the heaviness of the feelings. And nothing is more fun than having a good laugh with a friend.

I like having several good friends. Leslie is someone I can always talk to about anything. Breanna is a lot of fun and easy to laugh with. Mary and I love going to tennis classes together.

Friends help to bring out the many parts of me.

September 4

The opinion we have of ourselves
isn't just based on beliefs; it's also based on actions.
Marie Lindquist

Do you have a habit that gets you into trouble? I just can't stop interrupting others. No matter how many times I tell myself to keep quiet, I barge into someone else's conversation. I get a lot of dirty looks when I do this in front of either of my parents.

Sometimes I want to impress my friends more than I want to listen to them. I can be a show-off. But when I find out Sara had a bad day, I think, why am I showing off? I need to think of people around me as much as I think of myself.

My dad showed me how to do an "inventory" of my personality. He believes that until we know who we are, we can't change any part of ourselves, at least not permanently. Writing down what I catch myself doing tells me what my personality is like and what parts I'd like to change. My dad says we all have parts that need changing and that we are a "work in progress."

I like knowing who I am and what I can change.

All is well.

Grandmother Bellamy reminds my mom that "all is well" every time she begins to worry. And Grandma has to say it a lot. My mother worries every time my brother or I leave the house. Almost every time we all go away together, she has to go back in the house a couple of times to make sure she turned the coffee pot off or to make sure she didn't leave the water running somewhere. I worry sometimes, too—about school or about my friendships.

Do you have an idea of what "all is well" means? My grandma says it means that God is watching over our lives, and will do our worrying for us if we hand our worries over. We're wasting precious time that could be spent more productively. It's not that God's job is to worry, but that our burdens are lighter when we share them with God. When we worry over them, we're expending energy that we could use elsewhere.

I will turn my worries over to God.

September 6

Teaching is the royal road to learning.
Jessamyn West

There are many ways to teach. I used to think that teaching meant simply standing in front of a classroom introducing new ideas or reviewing old ones. Mr. Denny said that at every moment, everyone is teaching someone something valuable. For instance, even if you are argumentative, you're teaching all the people who come into contact with you to be wary. That may be an important lesson for them, but it isn't a lesson you want to be proud of having taught.

Watching my grandfather work in his yard has taught me a lot. Often he doesn't even speak. I have learned to appreciate watching birds by watching him watch them. I have learned how to plant delicate flowers, too, not by his explanations but by his movements. When I think about it, I probably have been taught most of what I've learned by simply observing others. I'd better not forget how often I am being observed.

I will teach only what I can be proud of having others learn from me today.

It is wonderful how quickly you get used to things, even the most astonishing.

Edith Nesbitt

The world has changed a lot since our parents were young. The changes since our grandparents were young are amazing. Can you imagine living in a world without television and computers? Not all change is in the technology surrounding us. You and I are changing all the time, too. If you doubt this, just look at your class picture from kindergarten.

My dad says that not all change is good, but it will come anyway. It is our job to learn how to adjust to change. My good friend Alison and I have always been in the same homeroom, and this year we're not, which means we can't be locker partners anymore. At first I was upset, but it has forced me to make some new friends. I had to ask someone I didn't know well to share a locker. I asked Libby, and she seemed happy that I did. Now I'm enjoying getting to know her better.

I will not shy away from change today. The change may bring me a surprising gift.

September 8

I think what weakens people most is fear.

Etty Hillesum

At a track meet last spring I was afraid I wouldn't have the strength to do two races. When I had the lead in the school play, I was a nervous wreck backstage before opening night. Each time my stepdad coached me. He said, "It's OK. Use your fear. Let it energize you."

Once I started running in the track meet, I felt great. I kept saying to myself, "I've practiced this a million times. I can do this." Once I started saying my lines, I got into my character. All my practice, the rehearsals, and my stepdad's coaching helped me walk through my fear. I felt it, but it didn't stop me from doing what I wanted and needed to do.

If I'm afraid today, I will tell someone about it.

Having friends is extremely important at any age.
Sheila Paul

To have friends, you need to be a friend. But are you sure you know what being a friend is about? I thought I did but learned otherwise when Mandy quit speaking to me. She had asked me to go to a movie with her. My mom said she would take us if Mandy's mom could pick us up after the movie. Then Brenda invited me to go to the zoo with her family. That seemed like more fun because I hadn't been there for two years. I told Mandy that I had changed my mind. Was she mad!

Mom and I talked about this when I got home from the zoo, and she said what I did was wrong, that I should not have dropped my plans with Mandy. Friendship is about being loyal. Loyalty means the other person can count on you to follow through. Are you always loyal to your friends?

I will not make a plan today that I can't keep.
I want to be a better friend.

September 10

Blaming others is acting irresponsibly.

My dad accuses me of making my brother the scapegoat whenever I get caught with my "hand in the cookie jar." When we don't want to accept responsibility for something we've done wrong or for something we didn't do when others were counting on us, we search for someone else to blame. He or she is "the scapegoat." "Having your hand in the cookie jar" means you were caught in the act, but you still try to deny that you are to blame.

Growing up means being willing to accept responsibility for all our actions. You might think this will be too embarrassing, but the interesting outcome is that you learn to make different choices about what you do when you know that you'll be held accountable. I sure hate getting blamed for something I didn't do. I can see how my brother feels the same way.

Even if I'm tempted to, I will not blame someone else for my actions.

Different opinions add color to a conversation.

Ramone S.

Sometimes I don't agree with what my friend is saying. Two people seldom think exactly alike. I guess that's actually as it should be. We learn from each other's opinions. A friend might change her opinion because of something you say, or vice versa. The give-and-take in conversation is what helps to teach all of us.

Having contempt for someone who has a different opinion is childish, but this is what I see Beth doing. Ever since Shelly moved to our school, Beth has made a point of belittling Shelly every time she says something that's not in agreement with Beth's viewpoint. It's hard to be around them. It should be OK to have differing opinions, shouldn't it?

I don't agree with my friends or parents about everything. That's OK as long as we show respect for each other.

September 12

Seeking approval is a futile exercise if done constantly.
Cara Halsema

Whenever my stepmother comes into my bedroom and tells me how nice it looks, I feel myself smiling inside. I am good about picking up my clothes and making my bed, and it means a lot to me when she notices.

I like compliments. I could be better about handing them out. I realized this when we discussed the topic of approval in Girl Scouts. Our leader said we can help others change their behavior by noting the things they do that are kind or helpful. She said that because most people like approval, they are more likely to repeat a behavior that someone has noticed and praised them for. Makes sense, doesn't it?

I will help someone strengthen a good behavior today by complimenting it.

Blessed are they who listen
when no one is left to speak.

Linda Hogan

Are you a good listener? You probably think you are. Most people do. But when you're listening to someone, is your mind absolutely there, or are flashes of other thoughts interfering? You may have to admit that you're wondering whether you'll be invited to the dance, or maybe you're worrying about being invited to someone's party.

Being fully attentive to the words of others isn't easy. It takes practice, like any skill. You have to practice to hit the hoop in basketball. You had to practice cursive writing for months before your writing became legible. Focusing on one thing at a time is one of the most important lessons we will ever learn. Today is a good day to practice.

How attentive can I be today?

September 14

Envy can prompt a person to work hard.

Most people are filled with envy when someone else has a quality or a possession that they would like. Envy almost seems involuntary. It just seems to be there.

My teacher says that envy can prompt a person to work harder to get whatever she perceives that she's lacking. Envy, then, can be good. But envy can push someone into talking behind someone's back as a way of getting even for not having what that person has.

Comparisons can serve us well only if we use them to push ourselves to work harder. For example, Terry is the fastest runner in my physical education class. My dad suggested that I time myself in short runs up and down our street. He said that if I put my heart and mind into it, I would be able to improve my speed. Perhaps I'll never catch up to Terry, but I'll run faster than I can now.

If I'm feeling envious today, I will attempt to develop in myself what I envy in someone else.

How we see an experience can change.

Perspective is how we see a situation. It is an individual thing, and it can change. Last week on my way to catch the bus, I fell and dropped my notebook. It skidded into a pile of leaves that were wet, and my history assignment got dirty. Mr. Hathaway said I could redo it and hand it in the next day. I was sure he would lower my grade for turning it in late. I was disgusted with my clumsiness. When I redid the paper, I realized I had left out a paragraph when I copied it from the first draft. If I had turned it in that way, I would have gotten a poor grade. I realized how lucky I was to have fallen down. See how a perspective can change?

My perspective on a book I've read might not be like yours at all. My dad's perspective on golf is not like my mom's. She hates golf, and my dad loves it. My sister's perspective on certain movies is much different from mine. I love horror movies. Perspective is an interesting concept. There is no right one or wrong one.

I wonder what will happen to change my perspective today.
I can respect my own perspective and other people's, too.

September 16

Patience is bitter, but its fruit is sweet.
Lida Clarkson

My mother puts sayings on our refrigerator as reminders of how to live. I like being the first to notice when she puts up a new one. I usually am. Mom likes that I take the time to read whatever is up there each day. The latest one is "Patience is a virtue."

I looked up synonyms for "virtue" on the computer. The one I like best is "honorable quality." Well, I knew that patience is an honorable quality, but knowing something and doing something are not the same. Rereading the saying every day helps me practice patience. That's the point, according to Mom. Learning to be patient improves my life in many ways. It helps me to show respect toward others, for one thing.

I can practice patience today.

Quiet minds can hear clear messages.
Robyn Halsema

Learning to be quiet will change your life. That's the message that came through in the essay Mrs. Phillips read to my history class last week. It was written by Anne Morrow Lindbergh, a famous author. She said that when our minds are quiet, we can hear messages from God that will make it easier for us to handle the hard stuff that happens. Her only son was abducted and killed when he was a child. That tragedy taught her to get quiet and to find healing in the quiet. She was no doubt willing to do whatever she needed to do to feel better. Her experience can certainly help us.

I hope that no one reading this essay will ever have to go through what Mrs. Lindbergh did, but all of us will have situations that are difficult. My family has had one. My dad decided he didn't want to live with us anymore. He said it was not my fault. He didn't blame my mom either. He just felt like he needed a different kind of life.

I will take some time to be quiet today. I want to hear the messages that are in my head and heart.

September 18

Self-pity slows a life down.

Feeling sorry for myself is such a drag. My older sister says I'm self-centered. That's why I feel sorry for myself so often. She told me to be aware of the world around me and make a list of all my blessings. All I had to do was think of the lady next door. She has been in a wheelchair most of her life because she fell out of a tree when she was young and injured her spinal cord. You might think she'd be feeling sorry for herself, but she isn't. She is one of the happiest people I know.

Attitude is everything. Mrs. Olsen shows this. She hasn't let her physical condition dictate how she's going to feel about any part of her life. She has a family and a good job at the library, and she recently went back to college. I have none of her problems and yet I feel sorry for myself. I can use Mrs. Olsen as a model for being more positive.

I will have a better attitude today. There is much I have to be grateful for.

Anger and worry are the enemies of clear thought.
Madeleine Brent

Our personality is defined by our thoughts. That sounds lofty, but its meaning is simple. Whatever you're thinking influences how you behave. If you're thinking that everyone in your math class is smarter than you are, you might avoid eye contact with the teacher, hoping she doesn't call on you. If you feel uncomfortable among new people, you will probably be quiet or even sneak out of the room or pretend to be lost in a good book. On the other hand, if you're thinking how lucky you are to be healthy and alive, you can probably laugh and talk with anyone sitting next to you.

Your thoughts are crucial to how you interact with people. Mom says one of the best ways to think more positive thoughts is to say affirmations, like, "I like myself. I am strong and courageous. I can do whatever I want to do." This may sound crazy, but it does help.

If I'm not happy today, I can change my thoughts.

September 20

I can change only myself,
but sometimes that is enough.

Ruth Humlecker

You cannot control other people. That's hard to accept when your younger brother has just grabbed the book you were getting ready to read. You can't control whether someone will be your boyfriend forever. You can't control how tall you'll get or what color hair you'll have or how many brothers or sisters you have. A lot of life is out of your control, isn't it? However, it helps to focus on all the things you can control.

You can control whether you drink alcohol or use drugs. You can control how much junk food you eat. How much you study for tests is under your control, and so is the tone of voice you use to answer your mother's questions. How helpful you are toward neighbors or friends is something within your control. Many important decisions are entirely up to you.

Wanting to control those things that are not ours to control is normal. I will practice walking away today.

You can rise above anger.

Being angry once in a while is normal. Parents get angry, too, of course. My dad has always said that anger isn't bad, but how it's expressed might be. He thinks that telling someone you're angry and then being willing to forgive them is the best way to deal with it. Admitting you're angry helps you to quit feeling it, he says. He learned this idea from a counselor.

But I'm not sure I want my anger to go away so easily, at least not all the time. Last week Priscilla told Chad that I wanted to be his girlfriend. I had told her that confidentially, and I was embarrassed that she told him. It feels right to be angry at her. She didn't even apologize for telling my secret. The problem is that Priscilla and Chad are in all my classes. I can't get away from either of them. Maybe I will have to talk to Priscilla about my feelings. What would you do?

If I'm angry and something is on my mind a lot, I will do the right thing and talk it over with someone or with the person I'm angry at.

September 22

Relationships are the way
we learn and grow and change.

I'm not sure I believe that everyone in my life has something to teach me. Teachers, for sure. And parents, too. Even older cousins and my brother and sister have shown me things. But when I think of Georgette, the most stuck-up girl in our class, I can't imagine what I am learning.

When I asked my dad about this, he told me a story about his first boss after he got out of college. His name was Mr. Brown and he was huge. My dad is short and felt intimidated. Mr. Brown was always waiting for him when he got to work and always criticized him for something he hadn't done right the day before. My dad grew to hate his job and Mr. Brown. He finally worked up the courage to tell Mr. Brown how he felt. To my dad's surprise, Mr. Brown apologized and said he hadn't realized how he was treating my dad. He was polite after that, and my dad learned how important it is to stand up for yourself. This was a valuable lesson early in his career. Mr. Brown was a good teacher in one way.

Difficult people teach me to balance thinking highly of others with thinking highly of myself.

Who thinks it just to be judged by a single error?
Beryl Markham

It is normal to make mistakes. We each make thousands of them. According to historians, the inventor Thomas Edison made five thousand attempts to develop the lightbulb before he succeeded. In other words, he made five thousand errors, but he never gave up. Each mistake simply eliminated one of his options.

It isn't likely that you're going to invent something that will have as profound an impact on our society as the lightbulb, but the important lesson is that mistakes are simply one way for us to learn what doesn't work. They don't say anything about our worth or intelligence. Mistakes, as long as they don't destroy our willingness to keep trying, are simply detours on our journey through life.

If I make a mistake today, I will learn from it. Mistakes are part of the learning process.

September 24

You cannot weave truth on a loom of lies.
Suzette Haden Elgin

Being absolutely truthful is an important value, and we would probably all agree that telling the truth is always the right thing to do. From childhood on, our parents, our teachers, and other adults in our life have stressed truthfulness. But we would probably all have to agree that on occasion, we don't tell the truth, at least not completely. Why is truthfulness harder in some circumstances than others?

Here's an example. Let's say the morning of the class field trip to the science museum, you wake up feeling sick. You pretend to feel fine because you know that if you admit you're sick to your mom, she will insist that you stay home. This might work out OK because sometimes a person feels lousy but gets better after having something to eat. Or you could feel worse as the day goes on. You could be exposing everyone in your class, even everyone at the museum, to your germs. Not being truthful can have an effect on dozens of unsuspecting people. It's hard to tell when it might be OK to "stretch" the truth, so telling it all the time is best.

I may think a "little white lie" is OK once in a while, but deviating from the truth can get me into trouble.

Resentment can become deeply rooted in us.

If someone mistreats you, do you think about ways to get back at them? Most of us want to punish someone who's been mean to us. I just read a book that showed how revenge gets you nowhere. In the story Hanna decided to get back at her cousin for a trick she had played on her. Mary had invited Hanna to a movie on a Saturday afternoon. Hanna showed up at the theater, but Mary's brother and his friends, not Mary, were there.

Hanna vowed to get even. The next week she asked Mary to meet her at the mall. When Mary got there, Hanna was not in their meeting place. Mary waited for an hour and then walked home. She vowed to get even. Can you see where this is going? The book ended with the question: Is there a better way to live than trying to get even?

Trying to get back at someone never gets us anywhere good. I want to treasure my friends, not make enemies of them.

September 26

Do you listen to your conscience?

Is there a tiny voice inside your head that nudges you to do or say the right thing? Mine speaks to me constantly. My dad says we all have a watchful conscience. It isn't always easy to listen to it, though.

The other day several kids were making fun of Adriana's new hairstyle. I wanted to join in because it was the popular kids and they were having a good laugh. But I took one look at Adriana's face and felt this twinge inside. I went up to Adriana and told her I loved her hair and walked to class with her. I felt a bit alone, but more in harmony with my conscience than I would have felt in that group of giggling girls.

My conscience will guide me to do the right thing.

Forgiveness is the act of admitting we are like other people.

Christina Baldwin

You have felt the forgiveness of your parents many times. Every time you've done something to upset them, they have eventually forgiven you. But how often do you forgive others? Try to remember the last time you got angry because a friend made fun of you or left you out. Were you able to forgive her? Forgiveness is seldom an easy thing to do.

The only way to learn forgiveness is to recall the times you've felt it from others and then act as if you feel it toward the person who has upset you. We can turn actions into good habits if we practice them, whether or not we believe in them fully. My mom says "acting as if" is the way she learned how to forgive. Try this. The first time someone bothers you today, say to yourself that you forgive them. See how you feel then. Mom says when she does this, she instantly feels different.

I will practice forgiving today by first saying to myself that I forgive someone.

It's a long trip to serenity.
I had better start right now.

Jill Clark

My mom taught me the Serenity Prayer. It's one she relies on dozens of times a day. It starts out by asking God for the wisdom to accept those things that are beyond our control. The example she used to explain it was when my dad decided he wanted a divorce. Mom said she prayed to be able to change his mind, but that prayer didn't work. Finally, she began to pray for the willingness to accept that he wanted a life different from the one he had been having with us, and she began to feel relief.

She said this prayer works for everyone who genuinely prays it. What I learned from her experience gave me the idea to try this prayer. I wanted the new girl in my classroom to be my best friend. I silently prayed for her to ask me to be her friend. She didn't seem to notice me. Finally, I prayed to be able to let her do whatever she wanted. When I did that, I was more myself and more natural around her, which felt good. Guess what? She invited me to her house within the week.

I'm so glad I have a prayer I can use throughout the day.

Prayer is not a science.

Mary McDermott Shideler

I have been thinking about prayer because my grandmother died last week. At her funeral, the minister said that if we ever wanted to talk with her, we could do so in the quiet spaces of our minds. He said our talks with her could be compared to prayers. He assured us she would hear us because her spirit had not died. It had simply gained freedom from her body.

I don't say prayers on a regular basis. At my cousin's house, a prayer is said before every meal. The first time I ate there, I took a big bite of chicken before I realized what I had done. Everyone pretended not to notice. When I suggested we say prayers before meals, my older brother gagged. Mom said that I had a good idea and I should come up with some ideas about what to say.

I will be quiet today and see if I can feel the spirit of someone special who has died.

September 30

Being noticed and praised for our accomplishments is very encouraging.

I enjoy praise for something I've done well. It makes me want to try even harder. Maybe it affects everyone that way. My grades have improved this year over last year, and I think it's partly because my parents have praised me for my grades and for my hard work.

Michelle fails many tests, but I know she's smart. I spend a lot of time with her outside of school, and she seems smarter than me in most things. Maybe her parents don't pay enough attention to how she's doing. We're only in the seventh grade, but my dad says we're already preparing for college. I think Michelle is overlooking that. I could praise her when she tries, and maybe that would help her feel like trying even harder the next time. Even if it doesn't, I'll know that I didn't hold back on expressing how great I think she is.

My parents praise me when I have earned the praise. I will work for it today, and I will freely praise the efforts my friends make.

October

Friendships soften the unfair moments in life.

An important reason for friendships is to have someone you can trust your secrets with. Mom says sharing your thoughts with a friend doubles your joy and cuts your unhappiness in half. I'm not sure just how that works, but I do know that when I'm upset about something, I feel better when I talk it over with Mom or a friend. Just having someone else to think about it with takes away some of the hurt.

Last week I found out that Corrie was having a party. All the girls in her jazz class were invited and they could bring a friend. I felt hurt that I wasn't invited. I talked to my older sister about it, and she said that sometimes things happen that aren't fair. That's just how life is. She promised to go out on the bike trail with me the day of the party, and I felt better.

Disappointments are easier to take
when I can share them with someone.

October 2

We can often do more than we think we can.

Meeting challenges head on isn't always fun, but you feel proud when you succeed. It's part of growing up. The most recent challenge I had was getting a flat tire on my bike when I was about five miles from home. I knew that my parents would be able to come and get me, but I sat down by the bike for a few minutes and had a great idea. I'd take the tire off and walk until I found a service station. I knew I could get air in the tire and maybe get a patch from someone in the service department. I was right. I got the tire back on and made it home before supper.

I told my family the story while we were eating, and my dad congratulated me for being able to solve my problem. He said it showed that I could think through a problem without panicking and that's the first step to succeeding in life. Second, he said that handling the problem myself rather than calling him or Mom to fix the situation showed I was creative and responsible. He then increased my allowance!

I can handle the challenges that come today if I don't panic.

*How desperately we wish to maintain
our trust in those we love.*

Sonia Johnson

Have you ever been a traitor? I am ashamed of how I treated Penny. She has been my best friend since third grade, and I told everyone at the lunch table a secret she had shared with me. I still can't believe I did that after I had promised I wouldn't tell. I apologized, but she wouldn't accept my apology.

I'm devastated. Have you ever been in a situation like this? What did you do? I will never share a secret ever again. I'm bewildered at how easily I let Penny's secret slip out. All the kids who heard it have been passing it on. I hope Penny will forgive me, but I bet she won't tell me a secret again.

I cannot undo the past. But I can make a commitment to myself to never tell someone's secret in the future.

October 4

Jealousy is all the fun you think they had.

Erica Jong

I am envious of my brother Troy. He's smart. He's strong and good in a lot of sports. And he has lots of friends. But the other day he was sitting in the living room and looking sad. I asked him what was wrong, and he said his girlfriend just broke up with him. He and I talked, and I realized he has his hard days and times, too. I felt close to him.

Even the people I think of as having everything are human and have their difficult times. It helps to remember that.

If someone else's life looks perfect to me, I know I'm not seeing the whole picture.

Truth, like surgery, may hurt, but it cures.

Han Suyin

There is no such thing as "kind of truthful." My reluctance to be absolutely truthful has always caused me problems. For example, last week, some kids from my history class decided it would be fun to play a practical joke on our substitute teacher. We sat in each others' seats to confuse her when she called on us. I wasn't so sure it was a good idea, but I went along. The joke backfired because the principal came in to observe her. He knew that the right kids were not responding to her questions. He's a good friend of my parents and told them about the prank. When they asked me about it, I lied and said I hadn't been involved. It was true that I hadn't thought it was a good idea, but I did participate. I was just as guilty as the rest of the kids, and I lied.

Not telling the truth can have consequences. Now I'm going to miss the school festival and the last three after-school programs. I wish all my friends had to miss them, too, but they admitted the truth right away and didn't get punished as badly.

I will be vigilant concerning the truth today. I understand how much trouble little lies can cause.

October 6

Willing to be oneself is not always easy.

Mary McDermott Shideler

On my bad days, I have an inferiority complex. I just don't feel that I'm as good as I should be at anything. I feel incompetent and doubt that my friends like me.

I discovered all this through a talk with my dad. He said these are just my bad days and I should try to remember all the good days, the days I feel confident. He gave me an affirmation to say over and over: "I am a child of God. I am as good as I need to be."

I'm changing my negative thoughts to positive ones today.

Everyone has special and unique talents.

Are you aware of the talent you were born with? Not many of us are. We all were born with particular talents, though. Some people say Mozart was the best composer who ever lived, and he began composing when he was a child. Eleanor Roosevelt, the wife of a former president, was a talented communicator. Her speeches influenced powerful people and helped to change many laws.

My dad is talented in mathematics and teaches at a college. My sister's talent is track. She is so naturally fast and graceful, it is fun to watch her run at meets, and she often wins. I haven't figured out my talent, but my dad said I should write a list of the things I love to do. He assured me that my talent was in that list somewhere.

I will make a list today. I want to know what my talents are.

October 8

I need help now!

Every girl reading this needs help sometimes. Even the president of the United States needs help in solving world conflicts. Everyone in my family needs help from each other. Since my dad had knee surgery, I help him around the house. My stepmother asks me to peel potatoes and carrots. She has so much to do when she gets home from work that my helping out counts for a lot, she says.

Sometimes we need help from others to solve our conflicts. My sister and I can't seem to solve our arguments without help from my dad. Before my mom and my dad got divorced, they went to a counselor for help. They got divorced anyway, but the counseling helped them to talk about their problems.

I will ask for help when I need to and offer help whenever I can today.

Opinions can imprison a person.

We form opinions from our experiences. Sometimes we have definite opinions. For example, maybe you're disgusted when a classmate cheats on a test and gets away with it. About other things, you may feel more ambivalence—you go back and forth on how you see something. I'm ambivalent about boys. My sister says this opinion will change.

Strong opinions can be hurtful. My aunt Linda is opinionated about religion. She thinks everyone should believe what she does about God and the church. My family is less rigid about God. We go to church most Sundays, but we don't go to Aunt Linda's church. She judges us harshly for that. It's obvious that Mom and Aunt Linda have been hurt. They hardly ever see each other anymore, which means I don't see my cousins.

I will make sure that the way I express my opinions is not hurting anyone today.

October 10

Now is the most important moment we have.

Karen Kirk

Don't borrow trouble. My grandmother, who moved in with us last year after her surgery, frequently tells Mom she is "borrowing trouble." I understood borrowing money or my older sister's favorite sweater, but I couldn't see how one could borrow trouble. I finally asked for an explanation. Borrowing trouble is worrying about the future. My mother does a lot of that.

Worrying about anything is a waste of time. But worse, if you spend the present worrying about something that might happen in the future, you will have missed your opportunity to experience your life right now. Grandma was successful in business for many years because she lived her beliefs. She didn't borrow trouble. Dad says that if more people lived by her philosophy, there would be fewer conflicts around the world and in each of our families.

I will stick to the present.

My parents told me I could do and be anything I really wanted. I believed them.

Molly McDonald

Courage is a wonderful quality. My mom says courage is the ability to do what I want and need to do despite feeling afraid or nervous. This summer I signed up for a seven-day canoe trip. I've always been interested in the woods and canoeing. I was nervous the week before: Would I be strong enough? Would I get homesick? Would I like my counselor and the other girls?

I had a great time and only a few moments of feeling homesick. When I came home, Mom and Dad said they admired my courage. I was proud of myself, too, and I loved being in the woods and on the water for so many days.

New experiences give me a chance to discover and exercise my courage.

October 12

*It's attraction, not promotion,
that persuades people to change.*

Setting a good example is important. I don't always realize this, but I know Thomas, my younger brother, imitates many of the things I do. Last week, he tried jumping down the bottom three steps into the basement and sprained his ankle.

Being a good example is a full-time assignment if you have little brothers and sisters. I envy Georgie. She doesn't have younger kids in her family. She does whatever she wants. I have heard her mother remind her older sister to set a good example for Georgie, though.

My parents say that we learn from one another constantly. They believe that the people we see each day are there because we are supposed to be learning from and teaching each other.

I will be kind and considerate today. I will be a model of the behavior I admire.

Why this fuss about death?
Try to visualize a world without death!
Charlotte Perkins Gilman

Mr. Franken, one of my former teachers, died yesterday. I was shocked. The whole school was. He was young. He had never been sick. He was running in the park and collapsed. An emergency squad was called, and he was pronounced dead right where he fell.

Death is mysterious. When one of my mother's aunts died, we talked about it a lot, but I still am confused about what actually happens to the person who is inside of the body we all see. Does that person quit thinking? Is that person immediately transported somewhere else?

Some people, depending on their religious beliefs, think nothing happens. Death is simply an ending to everything. There is no heaven, no angel, no God, no thought. I believe there is another world that we go to when we die, but I guess none of us will know for sure until we get there.

I'm glad I have someone to talk to about death.

October 14

Noticing how I awake can help me save the day.
Kelley Vickstrom

Cultivating a good attitude is like cultivating a garden. The weeds symbolize unattractive behaviors, and you have to pull them. You have to get their roots, too, or weeds will begin growing again. Dad says the process is the same for our "inner garden." We have to dig deep into ourselves to get rid of behaviors that bother others. Thinking about attitude this way makes changing it almost seem fun.

I have a tendency to notice what I don't get from my parents and compare it with what my brother gets. My mother says over and over again that we each get special things at different times. Sometimes my attitude is full of self-pity and resentment. I have to admit, when my mom points out all the things I get, it's a lot. I think having a good attitude means seeing my life in a more positive way.

I can change my attitude today.

The past is gone.

It's difficult to keep your mind on this very minute, isn't it? Not rethinking everything that happened yesterday feels impossible. It seems like my mind wanders to wherever it wants to. But my mind goes where I take it.

My parents have told me this countless times, but I keep dwelling on the past anyway. This wouldn't be such a problem except that there are a few sad times in my past, and when I spend all my time there, I don't notice what is meant for my attention now.

Dad says each day is an open book. Whatever gets written on each page is because of my effort. Each of us has some control over what our book will tell others when we've grown old. Or perhaps we can think of our life as a movie that's unfolding. You are the scriptwriter, the director, the star. What are you going to have yourself do?

I like thinking about my life as a book I'm writing or as a movie I'm directing.

October 16

Can you compromise?

Maturity is learning to compromise and feeling good about it. To compromise is to give in, at least part way. For instance, if you want to wear mascara and your mother says no, you agree to wear only lipstick for now. Satisfying each person is compromise.

Ted, my stepdad, said that the nations throughout the world would greatly benefit if they could compromise. The result of people not being able to give in is the death of millions of people around the world. What a terrible waste. Ted says that each of us can spread the idea of compromise by being willing to do it ourselves. Are you willing?

I am willing to give in today. Having everything my way isn't necessary.

We'd all like a reputation for generosity
and we'd all like to buy it cheap.

Mignon McLaughlin

How generous are you? We talked about this in class last week because of an argument. Nicole had brought a box of Girl Scout cookies to class to share because it was her birthday. However, she gave cookies only to her best friends, and Rachel called her stingy. By not sharing them with everyone, she had enough in the box to give each friend two, leaving five for herself. Mr. Quinn said generosity was a topic worthy of more discussion. He assigned us to ask our parents and brothers and sisters what they thought about the argument between Nicole and Rachel.

My dad said he thought Nicole had a right to do whatever she wanted with her cookies. Mom, who is a kindergarten teacher, said in her classroom the rule is you have to share with everyone. My older sister agreed. She said leaving certain kids out could hurt their feelings. She said that in her classes they often talk about the equality of all persons and how our views about equality come from learning to treat everyone with respect. What do you think about Nicole's decision?

I will think about generosity and equality today.

October 18

Peace can happen anywhere, anytime.

What image does the word "peace" bring to your mind? We have a statue on Mom's desk of a white dove carrying a twig in its mouth. Mom says the statue represents peace. She said Dad gave it to her many years ago after a big fight over which house to buy. Whenever we talk in history class about battles between nations, I always think of that statue. The dove seems so fragile.

Mr. Golding said that people have always been at war. The news on television shows how people are still at war. The history books document our wars. For hundreds of years one country has been in a struggle with another somewhere in the world. Mr. Golding suggested that we make a serious effort to get along with each other and pray and work for world peace.

I will work for peace in my friendships, my family, and the world.

Only in growth, reform, and change
is true security to be found.

Anne Morrow Lindbergh

We have dead bolts on our front door and back door for security. I wish I had a dead bolt on my bedroom door. My younger sisters got into my jewelry and fingernail polish last week while I was in school, and then I got into trouble for having left them out. It doesn't seem fair that I got blamed.

We discussed security at dinner that night. Dad agreed with Mom about the fingernail polish, but I learned that security doesn't just mean keeping things safe from the hands of little kids. Nor does it mean just being safe from someone who might try to break into our house. Security means feeling safe within yourself, not being overly self-conscious or fearful. Dad said he went into counseling when he was younger because he was insecure. Isn't it interesting how one word can stand for so much?

I will notice how many ways I value feeling secure.

October 20

Being safe can mean many things.

What does safety mean to you? Last week each of us had to write a short paragraph on what safety meant to us. About half of the class wrote something about keeping your doors locked. That's what I wrote. Our teacher wrote her paragraph on the board. Was I surprised. To her, safety meant believing that there was a God who watched over her in every situation she encounters. She said that because of her belief, she seldom worries about how any circumstance turns out.

I had never thought about safety that way. I do believe in God, but I never think about God keeping me safe. Perhaps I could adopt her philosophy and not be so worried. My grandmother laughingly accuses me of staying up late at night making up worries for the next day. Maybe I could try turning my worries over to God and relaxing into sleep more.

With God's help today, I will focus on feeling safe.

Have you made the decision to be happy?

My mother has some stationery that says "Have you made the decision to be happy today?" across the top of the page. She bought it because she thinks it's a good reminder to take responsibility for your own happiness. She considered ordering our family T-shirts with this printed across the front.

How can a person decide to be happy when something miserable has just happened? For instance, my purse got stolen last month in a restroom at school. How can I be happy about this? The point of the saying, Mom says, is that if I take responsibility for my loss, I'll realize I need to be more careful where I set my purse. If I'm more careful, I'll avoid some disappointment. Accepting happiness as my responsibility means I can have it whenever I choose.

Being accountable for my happiness today will be interesting.

October 22

The ability to choose puts human beings in control of their actions.

Mildred Pitts Walter

How many choices have you already made today? You made the one about picking up this book to read. You may have chosen which kind of cereal to eat for breakfast. I chose to eat eggs today. Realizing how many choices we get to make is important. My dad says that being allowed to make choices is an example of a democracy.

It doesn't always feel like a democracy at my house, however. Often my parents insist that I do only what they want. I didn't get to make the choice about which school I attended. Nor did I get to choose when I got my ears pierced. So far I've chosen not to smoke even though some friends do. My parents would ground me if I made that choice. The one choice I get to make every day is whether to have fun.

I will appreciate the choices I get to make today.

Fears don't have to take over our minds
unless we let them.

What comes to your mind when you think about fear? Miss Glass asked us to make a list of our fears. We stopped writing after five minutes. I had written thirty-seven things. Some classmates told how many fears they had written down. I suspected my list was longer than anybody's, and I kept quiet. I told my mom about this after school, though.

Mom assured me that being afraid is normal, but one characteristic of growing up is learning which fears are reasonable. One of my fears is that my friends will drop me if I don't use drugs with them when we get older. Because my dad's sister died from an overdose, drugs scare me. I promised Dad I wouldn't use drugs ever. Another fear is that our house will catch on fire. I don't know where this fear comes from, but I think about it almost every night at bedtime.

Are your fears reasonable? Talking them over with someone else helps.

October 24

Expecting the worst might trigger it.
Mary Hathaway

What kind of a day do you expect to have when you wake up? Dad says we often end up getting whatever we expect. He says some wise people even believe that each person creates her own experiences by the image in her mind. This doesn't mean that you can control what may happen to someone else, but it does imply that whatever image you carry in your own mind just might happen.

My dad gave me an example of how this happened to him. He was afraid when he got his first job. He imagined the boss was watching him constantly and waiting for him to make a mistake. He was so nervous that he ended up not paying close enough attention to the details of his job and got written up for carelessness three times. On the fourth time, he was fired. What he had feared would happen did. What he learned was that he probably would have gotten along fine if he had just enjoyed the job, paid attention to the details, and not been worried all the time about getting fired.

My mind can help me be peaceful. Or it can make me afraid.

Everything passes.

Ruthie Albert

When was the last time you looked closely at yourself in the mirror? I seldom notice how I've changed but my grandmother acts as though I've changed a lot every time I see her. It's probably because she's getting old and likes to remember me as a baby. But I am changing. All I have to do is see the pile of clothes laid out for the garage sale to be aware of my growth, and that's only one way I've changed.

I don't believe all the junk I used to believe. When I was little I wanted to be a secretary because my dad's secretary always gave me candy when Mom and I visited him at work. Now I want to be the manager. My dad says I'll be a tough one since I have strong opinions.

Some changes excite me and others make me feel sad. Mom says it's good to honor the mixed feelings—to talk about my feelings with her or a friend, or to write about them in my journal.

I will honor the changes in my life by taking time to notice and talk about them.

October 26

Everything that happens has a purpose.

All the moments in your life are important. By noon, you've forgotten the laughter at the breakfast table. By this weekend, you won't be thinking about the history assignment you left at home this morning. But the laughter and your forgetfulness matter. They're linked to the moments in the rest of your day. The laughter relieves tension. Some doctors say that nothing is better for health than laughter. The assignment you left at home can be a good reminder, in a roundabout way, to plan ahead. If you had put the paper by your jacket before sitting down to breakfast, you might not have forgotten it.

Every circumstance serves an important purpose. We can listen closely to the events in our lives and pick up hints, reminders, and affirmations. Our lives hold a lot of meaning.

I have a lot I can learn each day. I will be attentive to what today has to teach me.

There are persons who have some parts like me,
but no one adds up exactly like me.

Virginia Satir

You are unique. Just as no two snowflakes are alike, even identical twins are not identical. Some people believe that our uniqueness signifies how necessary each person is to the circle of humanity. Those who believe in God would even say that God made sure each one of us is different, at least slightly, to complete all the world's tasks. Do you know what your tasks are?

It doesn't matter why we're unique; what's important is that we are. What's also significant is how similar we are within our uniqueness. Even if we don't mirror each other physically, our feelings and thoughts are often alike. What discourages one person often discourages another. What angers me probably would anger my friends.

I will appreciate the ways I mirror my friends and the ways I am unique.

October 28

Everyone feels lonely from time to time.

Are you often lonely? It happens to me sometimes when I can't find anyone to hang out with. Or if my mom and my dad are upset with me, I sometimes feel lonely at home. One thing I have learned is to read a book, play the piano, or go for a bike ride. The loneliness often turns into a peacefulness inside.

My grandmother says she gets lonely since my grandfather died. What helps her is writing letters, knitting, or calling me up. She says it's good to know how to reach out to others when we're lonely and to develop ways to enjoy being alone.

If no one is available the next time I'm lonely,
I will find a way to have a peaceful time alone.

Conflicts are opportunities to learn.

I get into a conflict with a friend nearly every day. Miss Waverly pointed this out to my parents when I was in second grade and I haven't changed much in six years. I can't seem to give in when others have different opinions. Dad said conflict is natural. He and Mom have a lot of disagreements. The important thing about conflict is that you can learn to have it without letting it ruin your day or a friendship, but you have to be willing to compromise.

I don't cause every conflict I'm in. I'm the innocent person once in a while, but I do cause some conflicts because I'm too bossy. Learning how to compromise is a skill that ranks up there with learning geometry and geography. We will have to be willing to compromise for the rest of our lives if we hope to have friends. I guess this is what my parents do. They are friends in spite of their conflicts.

I will try to compromise today before I get into a conflict.

October 30

Are you the kind of friend you want others to be?

When I was younger, I had a friend who was taller than me. I envied her ability at the high jump. The neat thing about her height was that she could reach the top shelf in the lunchroom, where the desserts always were. I made sure we were always in line next to each other, and when I was late to lunch, she usually noticed and rushed over to me and offered to reach whatever I needed. Mom says this is a real example of friendship.

I try to be a good friend to my younger sister in the second grade. She is struggling to learn her subtraction facts. I have been practicing with her two or three nights a week. It makes her feel just as happy as having Jennie for a friend made me feel.

Being a good friend takes little more than a desire to be kind and thoughtful.

How much do you value companionship?

How kind are you to your friends? If you're not very kind, you have some important work to do. What we offer to others comes back to us. My stepmother says this is a principle of life that never fails. If you're considerate, you can expect tons of kindness to come back to you.

My stepmother has a whole bunch of beliefs that are similar to this one. She says that we are "on assignment" to learn certain things from one another. My friend Jesse is the oldest of five. She can't do a lot of things because her mom is so busy with younger kids. This makes me appreciate all that my mom does for me. Often Jesse does things with us, which she really likes. I have fun at her house in a special way. Her little sisters are so cute, and I love to read stories to them. That makes me feel special.

Sharing experiences, interests, and talents with friends enriches my life.

November

Practice never makes perfect
but you won't even be good without it!
Sandra Lamberson

Everything you want to be good at takes practice. Even activities you learned as a little girl, something as simple as making your bed and brushing your teeth, are only as good as you make them through practice. I always thought that adults were just good at certain things. I never saw my dad practice driving the car, for instance. But he says that years of driving to work and around town is what made him a good driver. Every trip was practice. I think my big brother must need some more practice driving. He had an accident last week backing out of our driveway.

It's good to know that practicing isn't just for kids, and that everybody is helped by it. Now it doesn't seem so unfair of our basketball coach to make us run the length of the gym ten times every afternoon after practice. She says it's for our own good, like eating broccoli.

I'm willing to practice all kinds of things today.
Improving at activities I like is fun.

November 2

Opportunities for growth come at us every minute.

Everything that happens in your life is an opportunity to show respect, express love, learn something new, or offer help. This might not seem possible a lot of the time. Like last week, when I was arguing with Tammy over which video to watch. She wanted to watch *The Sound of Music* for the hundredth time, and I said no way. Tammy got so mad she went home. My aunt heard us arguing and suggested that giving in might have been a better way for me to handle the situation.

It isn't easy to figure out when to be assertive and when to give in. Aunt Karen has chosen to always give in. She says it feels better to her in the long run because most arguments are about selfishness and control. Feeling peaceful makes her happier. When she feels inner happiness, she has more fun regardless of what she's doing.

I can take time to consider whether arguing for my way is worth it today.

Noble deeds and hot baths
are the best cures for depression.

Dodie Smith

A special report on depression was on television the other evening. The main message was how much more often it is affecting children of all ages than in the past. My parents watched the report because my sister, Julia, who is two years older than me, seems depressed. She cries easily and gets frustrated when something goes wrong.

After the report was over, we sat around the dining room table and talked about it. Each of us asked Julia how we could help her. She admitted she had been worried herself. Things that used to feel easy to her were feeling hard. Getting up and going to school was feeling hard. Her best friend just moved away, and she didn't make the track team. I could tell she appreciated our concern. Mom and Dad are going to take her to a counselor who knows about teenage depression. We all felt closer after this discussion.

People who are depressed can get better.
There's a lot of help available.

November 4

What is so certain of victory as patience?

Selma Lagerlöf

Most people want what they think they need immediately. When your mom asks you to clear the dinner table or make your bed, she doesn't mean when you get around to it. She wants it done now. When you want help with your math or the science project due Friday, you want attention now. You probably even get irritated if your dad has already offered to help your brother with his homework. Impatience is common.

One sign of maturity is learning to be patient. My aunt who is a writer tells me that it takes patience to be a good writer. She has to revise the stories many times. She says many good things require time, and that means we need to have patience. Some of the best rewards come slowly.

I will work on patience today.

When we are all wrapped up in ourselves,
we present a very small package to others.
Georgette Vickstrom

Angie is the most self-centered girl in our class. She moved to our neighborhood from a private school and thinks she's smarter than any of us. She brags all the time about all the activities they had at her old school that our school doesn't have. She's always talking about what she does and wants to do as if she is far more interesting than any of us.

Mom explained that people who seem selfish and self-centered may be trying to cover up their insecurity. I try to understand this, but it's just plain hard to be around her. Angie is a good reminder of how important it is to be interested in each other—to ask questions and listen.

Listening and paying attention to each other are important parts of friendship.

November 6

We never have to make a decision alone.

I'm confused. I live with my grandmother, and my mom wants me to spend the weekend at her house, but my dad wants to take me on a business trip to California for a few days. My friends all say they would go to California, but I've been there, and I haven't stayed with my mom since she moved into her new house. What would you do?

Making decisions can be difficult, especially when people's feelings are involved. I don't want to hurt anyone. My grandmother says I need to do what would make me the happiest. She has told me many times that my parents will understand my choice.

Many decisions are hard to make. Talking over difficult decisions with another person always helps.

If I need to, I can always get help making a decision.

Remember to be grateful.

I quickly forget what's really important. I'm seldom thankful for my older brother. I'm preoccupied with all the junk I want and don't have. Or I envy the good luck of others. Yesterday, I wasted almost an hour lying on my bed dreaming about what I would buy if I won the lottery. I would get all the clothes I want, then the jewelry, and then a red convertible, even though I won't be able to drive for three more years. In my imagination I filled up my room with things.

Being grateful for what I do have doesn't seem important. My dad told me a story about his childhood that he hoped would make me think. On his seventh birthday, his grandparents surprised him with a red bike. Immediately after opening his presents he took off on the bike. When he got back, his grandparents were gone. They had left for home, but his grandfather was killed in an accident on the way. Dad hadn't even said good-bye. Remembering to be grateful for the people who matter to us while they are alive is something he's never forgotten.

I'm grateful for all I have, especially the people in my life.

November 8

Good feelings can be cultivated like a rose garden.
Rosemary Brown

What gives you good feelings? We discussed this in class today because Brenda brought a treat for her birthday. She made chocolate cupcakes with coconut frosting. They were delicious. She told us it made her feel good to bake treats for others. The teacher asked us to think about what makes us feel good and plan to talk about it in class tomorrow.

What makes me feel good is getting high scores on exams, especially when I've studied hard. My mom feels best when she's received a promotion at work. My dad says he feels good when he looks at all of us kids. He's proud to be our father. I thought most kids would feel good to get good grades, but my brother and sister didn't give that example. What would be your answer?

I know what feels good to me. I will work to have some good feelings today.

Anger clearly needs expression.

Holly Wright

I need to think about how I handle my anger. It has never made a situation better. When I got mad, I used to complain that I couldn't help it. Laura, my stepmom, said that was nonsense, that nobody was in charge of my feelings but me. She offered to help me with healthy ways to handle my anger.

Laura said the first thing I needed to explore was what kinds of situations trigger my anger. Avoiding those situations might not be possible, but she was willing to help me figure out how to handle them in a new, more creative way. I realized I most often get angry when I don't get my way. Laura said that might call for constant creativity. Otherwise, she said I could decide to believe that everything turns out the way it should. "My way" would be the "right way" only some of the time.

Anger is not bad. I might need to work on how I handle it, though.

November 10

Opportunity doesn't discriminate.
Eleanor Atchley

Every time a situation doesn't turn out the way I had hoped, I have a chance to celebrate that something better is coming for me. This didn't make much sense to me when my older sister suggested it, but I am beginning to believe it. She said believing this has made her happier than she could have imagined.

She reminded me of the time I had planned to see a movie one Saturday, but Dad said he expected me to help him clean the basement. I was willing to help, but I wanted to do it early, before the movie. The glitch was that he got called in to work. He still wasn't back by midmorning. I started without him, and about the time I finished cleaning the first corner, he came home and was so pleased that I had started without him, he said I could go on to the movie. He gave me extra money for treats, too.

I will look for my opportunities today. Sometimes they come in surprising ways.

Revenge hurts both sides.

Being cruel is never justified. You might think that revenge is OK, and you might see your parents or friends acting in ways to get revenge, but it's wrong. "Turning the other cheek" is always the right reaction to a person who has treated you unjustly. Are you familiar with that expression? It's from the Bible. It means that when a person has treated you badly, you forgive her, and even allow her to wrong you again if she must. The right reaction is to ignore her behavior. This is not easy. We always want to pay the other person back. The problem with revenge is that the conflict never ends. First you're getting back at her, then she's getting back at you.

It's not easy, but our lives are less disrupted if we learn to forgive others' bad behavior. Walking away from an argument or a nasty person doesn't mean we are cowards.

I can turn the other cheek today if I make that my choice.

November 12

Envy can be so painful.

It's not unusual to envy others. Everyone is envious sometimes. Maybe you think the members of your favorite rock band are never envious. But they are. They have all the same feelings that you and I have.

What can you do with your envy if it troubles you? What I've learned is that making a list of all the wonderful things in my life takes my mind off the situation or person that triggers my envy. My mind can't be on two things at the same time.

Sometimes what I envy is someone who has accomplished something that I would like to pursue in my life. That tells me that I can use envy as a light to direct me where I need to go. The key is to change my thoughts from envy to gratitude for something I have.

I don't have to be envious. That's not difficult, but it takes practice.

Complimenting others is a way of making the world a happier place.

How do you feel when you are praised? Just last week, Mrs. Hawthorne, our new neighbor, brought a plate of oatmeal cookies to our door and told Mom they were especially for me because I had helped her shovel her driveway after the big storm. Mom gave me a big compliment, too. She said she felt proud that I was her daughter. She hadn't even suggested I offer to help Mrs. Hawthorne.

I've noticed that when I praise my younger sister for how she cleaned our room or scored at her soccer game, she can't help but smile. You can help someone be happier each day simply by noticing what that person does well and praising him or her for it. My grandfather believes spreading around happiness in small doses like this could change the world.

I will praise a few people today for behaviors I recognize as kind.

November 14

You don't have to tolerate bullying.

We all know a bully. The one who comes to my mind is Roger, the newest boy in middle school. He picks on other kids and hasn't made a friend yet. He keeps chasing my younger sister every time she walks by his house. She doesn't even want to walk that way anymore. I sure don't want to be thought of as a bully.

My mom called up Roger's mom, who was upset by her son's behavior and said that he would be over to apologize soon. Sometimes we need help from our parents or a teacher with trying to stop a bully. My mom says she remembers the bully in her elementary school and wishes that she and her friends had stood up to him. She is convinced that his conscience must still be heavy because he was mean to so many kids.

I don't want to be a bully or be bullied. There's always a caring adult around who can help me with this.

Friendship makes every experience better.

Denise is my best friend. Her older brother Cohen got his driver's license last month and can take us to the movies at the mall. But having a best friend is about a lot more than getting rides! It means you have someone to share your feelings with. It's good for adults to have a best friend, too. Heather is Mom's. When Dad moved to an apartment, Mom talked to Heather on the phone at least once a day. Some days she called her more than once. It really helped her.

Having someone to share your worries with keeps worries from taking over your thoughts and your life. Having a friend to talk to cuts your worries in half. Getting the worries out of your head allows you to notice the good experiences that are just waiting to happen. I'm lucky that I have a best friend. Do you?

Today I will show my best friend how much I appreciate her.

November 16

What did you really see?

Last Saturday I saw a terrible accident at the intersection near my house. The ambulance came, along with the police. Two people were rushed to the hospital. Glass was everywhere. I haven't been riding my bike near that intersection since then because I don't want a flat tire.

Mother saw the accident because she was backing out of the garage to go grocery shopping. When we talked about the accident at dinner, I was surprised to hear how she described it. She blamed it on the red convertible. She said the kids in that car were speeding. I saw the old station wagon pull right in front of the convertible. Dad said that's how perception works. No two people see anything exactly the same way.

Wars between countries, even arguments between two people, are fought over differing perceptions. Being willing to see something another way could create a more peaceful world.

I will remember that whatever I see, another person might see it another way.

Remember the Golden Rule:
Do to others as you would have them do to you.

Are you a secretive person, one who is often whispering to a friend about things you want no one else to know? Making a big deal about having a secret can make other kids feel left out, and that can hurt. If you are sharing a secret with a friend and making a big deal of it in front of someone, you may be causing unnecessary pain. Is this what you want to do?

Likewise, if you talk out loud in front of others who aren't included in something you're planning to do, that can hurt. You know you don't like it when someone does it to you.

In choosing how to act today, I will consider the feelings of those around me.

November 18

It is almost impossible to throw dirt on someone without getting a little on yourself.

Abigail Van Buren

Being a gossip is never a good idea. I learned this the hard way. I told a whole group of girls in my class that my neighbor had been arrested. I had assumed this after seeing a police car in her driveway early that morning. The rumor spread quickly. When I got home from school, my mother was on the phone hearing the rumor from Heidi's mom. She glared at me because she knew I was the one who told the story. The truth was that Mrs. O'Connor's oldest son had been injured in a car accident and the police were there to inform her. My mother said I owed Mrs. O'Connor an apology.

Rumors spread so easily. Worse than that, the rumor got distorted and bigger. By the time it had reached my mother, Mrs. O'Connor had been arrested for shoplifting and was going to jail. My mom stopped the gossip in its tracks because she had talked to Mrs. O'Connor before the call from Heidi's mom. Do you spread gossip?

I won't pass along a story about anyone today unless I know all the facts. Even then, if the story isn't kind, I will be quiet.

Ridicule is mean-spirited.

Being ridiculed hurts. I know from experience. Our history teacher assigned us to read a biography and give a report on a famous person. I chose the writer George Eliot. I'm such a procrastinator that I never got around to reading much of the book, but I skimmed it, figuring I could make up some details and the class wouldn't know the difference. What I hadn't counted on was that Rhonda would choose the same person to report on.

I stood up and started talking about George and *his* life and *his* novels. No one said anything until I finished. Rhonda raised her hand and informed the class that George was only a pen name. George was actually a woman. Everyone burst out laughing. I should have worked harder on the paper, but everyone making fun of me really hurt.

I will remember that I don't like to be ridiculed if I'm tempted to join in making fun of someone today.

November 20

Unkindness almost always stands for the displeasure that one has in oneself.

Adrienne Monnier

Pam has been a friend of mine for a short time. I remember the day she moved to our neighborhood. I had just gotten my new mountain bike. She had a bike almost like mine. We rode over to the park, and I introduced her to all my friends. She was friendly at first, but what began to happen surprised me. It took me awhile to understand what she was doing, but finally I caught on. She didn't want me to be friends with anyone but her, so she criticized everyone constantly. Pretty soon I was seeing only their negative traits, too.

Having hardly any friends isn't fun. I still like Pam, but I miss Gina and Holly and Kim. We used to ride our bikes together almost every warm day. I liked it better when I focused on the positive traits of my friends, and now that I see this more clearly, that's what I'm going to do. I don't need to shrink my heart to be Pam's friend. There's room in my heart to like all these friends.

I don't need to be unkind to anyone to be a friend to someone.

Fear complicates one's life.

Teri Faricy

A book that my mother reads every morning helps her feel love for all the people in her life rather than fear about what they might do. She has been reading this book over and over, she said, because it is too easy to be afraid rather than trust that everything will ultimately work out for the best. She told me that there's no shame in feeling afraid. Are you often afraid?

My mother defined fear as lack of faith. She said that faith is believing God is with us in everything that happens, and if we rely on God—on a Higher Power in the universe—we'll get through every single experience that comes to us. These experiences can teach us something that we need to know. What am I supposed to learn from having my bike stolen twice? Mom says if I think about this for a while, I will understand.

I will allow my faith to be stronger than my fear today.

November 22

There are two sides to every issue.

Ayn Rand

Being willing to compromise when you have a difference of opinion about how to play a game is a good habit to form. In fact, compromise is usually a good idea when two people are arguing over anything. It often means taking turns in getting your way, and that might not seem as much fun as getting your way every time, but it's fair and it saves having unnecessary, extended arguments.

Compromise has another meaning, too. Let's say your friend asks if she can copy your homework. You don't want to let her because you value honesty and letting her copy isn't honest, but she's someone you've wanted to be better friends with. What do you do? Giving in to her request means compromising your values. Have you ever been faced with the dilemma of someone wanting you to compromise a value that is important to you? Asking an adult to help you think through a situation like this might be a good idea.

I can learn to compromise when it's healthy to do so and still be true to myself.

Hey, let's talk.

Being a good communicator means you're willing to discuss what's on your mind. It also means being an attentive listener no matter who's speaking to you and interacting willingly in the lives of the people around you. Communication is a necessary ingredient in any healthy relationship.

When the topic of communication came up in one of my classes last week, I had the chance to impress Mr. Bradley with all my thoughts. I didn't tell him I learned them from my stepfather. He probably figured that anyway. I've seen Mr. Bradley speak to him at football games many times.

I'm glad I've learned the importance of good communication. I will practice what I've learned today.

November 24

The one with the primary responsibility
to the individual's future is that individual.
Elizabeth Cady Stanton

Do you know what it means to be accountable for all your actions? My parents said that we needed to have a talk about this because I blame others for many of my mistakes or errors in judgment. I honestly didn't think they were right. I was sure that I acted responsibly. But I was wrong.

For me to see what he was talking about, my dad recounted some times when he didn't accept responsibility for his actions. I suddenly realized that I hadn't taken responsibility for dozens of things, many of them small, like not admitting I erased some phone messages by mistake. Mom said that I need to change or others will begin to not trust me, and because the qualities, the good and the bad, that we develop as kids stick with us for a lifetime.

I'm quite sure I will want to be considered a worthy adult.
What I do today contributes to the adult I will become.

When we yield to discouragement,
it is usually because we give too much thought
to the past and to the future.

Saint Therese of Lisieux

I envy Leah because she acts so confident in everything she does. She's an excellent student. In history class she gets an A on every assignment. Next to her scores, mine are dismal. I work hard, but I can't retain all the information. Sometimes I feel hopeless. Thank goodness, Sylvia, my stepmother, understands.

Sylvia says it's so important not to compare ourselves with others. We all have strengths and weaknesses. She says I need to switch my focus. If I focus on trying to be like Leah, I might always be discouraged. But if I focus on learning, working hard, and doing my best, then I'll notice more feelings of hope and satisfaction.

I will focus on encouraging, not discouraging, myself today.

November 26

Defects are simply bad habits
waiting to be discarded.

Josephine Casey

The saying on a poster in my bedroom is "I may not be perfect, but a few of my parts are excellent." My foster dad gave this to me after I got caught skipping school. I had expected to be grounded, but he said my shame over what I had done was enough punishment. He said that I had disappointed my classmates more than him. They had counted on me being there for a big game. I'm the best hitter on our class softball team, and we had a challenge game with the seventh grade. Guess who lost.

I skipped school a lot before getting placed in this home. These parents are kind, and they talk to me almost every day about making changes in my behavior. I want to earn their praise. I'm not sure why my old ideas take over my mind sometimes, but they do. My foster dad said not to dwell on what I did, but to make a promise to myself that I won't do it again. He said that remaking the promise every day is how a new behavior becomes a good habit.

I will work on strengthening a good habit today.

Respect is the basis of all good friendships.

I want to always show respect for people close to me and far away. Showing respect for the people in my family means treating them kindly, the same way I want to be treated. I want to show respect for people of all cultures, too. Remember reading about slavery in school? Men and women and children native to Africa were deprived of their freedom and treated like animals because of their dark skin. They were not respected for the ways in which they were different.

Respect yourself as well. Having self-respect means that you value your own personality and opinions. Be aware of your thoughts, because they usually determine what you are going to do and say. Feeling good about who you are every time you speak is having self-respect.

I will show respect for everyone I meet wherever I go today.

November 28

Friendships shift and change;
but caring can be constant.

Veronica and Rochelle used to be inseparable, but last week they got into a huge argument. Mr. Gentry said that personalities change as people mature and best friends sometimes go their separate ways. Friends might begin to argue as interests or opinions change.

It's hard and sad when this happens. Mr. Gentry reminded us that even when changes make a friendship more distant or uncomfortable, each person can still care about the other.

Even if a friendship of mine is shifting, I can honor my friend for all that she is and all that she has given me.

God loves unconditionally.

Unconditionally—that's how God loves you. God has set the example, but most of us can't imitate the behavior. It's more common to seek ways to *not* love another person. To love unconditionally means being able to absolutely ignore a person's faults or how a person looks. It's being able to overlook how a person behaves toward you or other people. What it means is total love, regardless of every possibility for not feeling love.

Loving unconditionally seems impossible, doesn't it? Maybe you could talk about this idea with your family or friends. It's hard not to let annoyances or differences stand in the way of loving a person. Even (or especially) your mom and dad are hard to love sometimes. When my dad divorced our family, I hated him. Mom said it was OK to have my feelings but hoped I wouldn't hate him forever. Of course, I don't hate him anymore, but I'm not so sure I love him unconditionally. Do you know what I mean?

It's impossible to completely follow God's example of unconditional love, but I will keep it in mind today.

November 30

Impulsively reacting when others upset us doesn't ever help the situation.

What comes to your mind when someone does something mean to you? I used to want revenge until my foster mom had a talk with me about considering the consequences before acting. That got me thinking. For example, last week Ted ran over my history assignment with his bike. I had worked on it all weekend. First, I wanted to knock him off his bike. Then I wanted to kick him.

Fortunately, I remembered to take a few deep breaths. I did a fast-forward in my mind, and I could see that knocking him down would only escalate into a bigger fight. I went on to school and explained to Mr. Vasquez what had happened and told him I would bring in another copy tomorrow. Luckily, I had saved the report on the computer. It felt good to stay calm. Fighting is never fun.

I am in charge of what I do today.

December

Humor is such a strong weapon,
such a strong answer.

Agnes Varda

I like hanging out with Rose and Elena. They know hundreds of jokes. I always try to sit close enough to them at lunch to hear their latest ones. I love to laugh at jokes, and those two girls are known throughout the school for laughing a lot and being a lot of fun.

Laughter feels so different from every other experience. It helps me forget whatever might be upsetting me. Since last week I've been sad because my stepdad decided to move back to the town where he was born. Mom's sad, too, but he couldn't get a good job here. He promises to come back every weekend, but I'll miss all the times we played Scrabble or rummy in the evenings after my homework was done. Listening to a great joke helped me forget my loneliness for a minute today.

I will look for a reason to have a good laugh today.

December 2

Listening to a friend is like giving her a gift.

The act of listening is significant. First, you can always learn something. For instance, when my brother was talking about his science project during dinner last night, I learned some facts about electricity. I plan to share these in my science class. Second, you're given an opportunity to honor another person by your willingness to listen. Third, some people believe that through listening we will hear special messages that are meant to make our own lives happier. These guardian angels speak to us through the voices of others. What do you think?

I'm not as good a listener as I might be. My mind wanders. But I do know how much I love being listened to, and I would like to do that for others.

I will honor the special people in my life today by listening and paying attention to them.

Changing myself is hard.
Changing others is impossible!

I used to try to change my little brother. He was always in my room, messing up my bookcase or pulling the blankets off my bed right after I made it. Mom suggested I keep my door closed if I want to keep Tommy out. I figured she should keep him out. Nothing changed. He kept coming in and I kept yelling at him and complaining to Mom.

Last year I finally realized why I couldn't get Tommy to do what I wanted. I learned this in a strange way. My dad was constantly nagging me to do my homework someplace other than the living room floor. I heard his complaints, but I loved doing it in front of the television. And I didn't think he really cared. I thought he just liked to yell once in a while. One night Tommy was eating a Popsicle when he ran through the living room. He tripped on one of my books and ruined my homework. Guess who doesn't do their homework on the living room floor anymore?

Deciding to change how we do something is harder than it seems at first. I will concentrate on this idea today.

December 4

Are you paying attention
to the events in your life?

Life is confusing, isn't it? Good friends move, relatives die, families change. My dad believes my girlfriends are in my life to help me survive the changes that confuse me. I'm glad Mary Beth is a friend. She cried with me when my cat got killed. Anna always makes me laugh, and Liz and I love working on art projects together.

Dad says I'm helping other girls, too. When someone seems depressed or worried, I can be gentle. When someone is scared, I can share something that has scared me, too. The main thing to remember is that we need each other, and the more we pay attention to one another, the more we can help each other out.

Friendship is a wonder-filled, two-way journey.

Envy poisons.

I hate it that Hannah moved here last year. Everyone has put her on a pedestal; even the teachers seem to like her better than all the rest of us. She is the center of attention in every class and every activity. I used to be, at least once in a while. Are you ever envious?

I think Mrs. Russo, the homeroom teacher, has an idea how I feel about all the attention Hannah gets. She suggested we have a class discussion about envy. I am too ashamed to admit how envious I feel. I know other girls envy her, too. Would you be able to admit your feelings in a situation like this? If you couldn't admit them, what would you do with them?

If I'm feeling envious today, I will talk it over with someone I can trust.

December 6

Loyalty is always right but not always easy.

Being loyal to who we are means that what we feel inside is the way we act outside. Let's say that in your family it's important to say a prayer before a meal. But when you're at a friend's house, you notice they don't take a moment to pray. They dig right in to their food. That's OK, but it's still important for you to silently say a prayer. This is an example of being loyal to your values.

Being loyal to friends might mean that when you tell Megan you'll spend Saturday with her, you don't change your mind when Lisa invites you to a movie. You can be counted on to do what you've agreed to do. Loyalty is standing up for your friends and being happy for them in their successes.

Loyalty makes my friendships strong.

Needing to win is a sign of immaturity.

My older brother gets furious when he loses at cards. A favorite game in my family is 500 rummy. We play it almost every weekend, especially if my grandmother comes over. Josh will want to play, and before we're halfway through, he's stomped out of the room. He's a poor sport.

I'm lucky that I don't feel the need to win every game. People who have to win all the time don't seem happy. The new girl in our neighborhood is a lot like Josh. She even swears if we don't play certain games her way. My friend Marty and I often pretend we're busy when she invites us to come to her house.

It's fun to play games with friends, and winning and losing is part of it all.

December 8

Chance is the first step you take,
luck is what comes afterwards.

Amy Tan

My stepmother got so sick last week she went into the hospital. The same day, my dad got laid off from work. That meant he had time to go to the hospital, but that was the only good part of that situation. Next, my cat ran away. Snuggling with the cat had always given me hope, and I needed a lot of that. My little brother was scared, too.

When everything seems to go wrong, what can you do? After Dad got home from the hospital one night, we sat and talked. He could tell I was worried, but he said his parents had told him when he was young that help will come if we believe in the power of prayer. Dad said it would be good for me to put my attention on my younger brother. Diane and he were going to be fine.

Prayer can help in any circumstance. I will pray today.

Mean-spirited people have very few friends.

Thelma Elliott

We can never take back something we've said. We can apologize. We can promise to never say something mean again. But whatever we said is history. What follows is remorse.

It's easy to avoid feelings of remorse. Think through what you're going to say before you say it. Do you know people who always seem kind? Are they different from you? Not really. Maybe they have made a promise to themselves to be kind, no matter what. If we pause before responding to a situation, or if we use a pleasant tone of voice when we start a conversation, we'll have more friends and no remorse. We can never take back something we've said, so it's important to make sure we really want to say what comes out of our mouths.

I will take charge of my words today. That way I won't have to be sorry.

December 10

In a total work, the failures
have their not unimportant place.

May Sarton

Not being good in a sport or a school subject can be frustrating, especially if it's something you've practiced or studied really hard. I've always admired my cousin Nick. He didn't make the basketball team in ninth grade, in part because he was too short. But he loved the game so much he practiced every day and made the team in the tenth grade. By his senior year he was a star on the team, and we all watched his team play at the state tournament. It was so exciting!

It inspires me that Nick didn't let his early failures stop him from doing what he loves to do. I try to remember this when I face small failures.

I will learn from my failures and allow them to deepen my own commitment to what I want to do and be.

Helping others is generally a good choice.

Are you willing to help others when they ask? Be honest. Has your mom ever asked you to pick up your clothes or clean up the bathroom after you've showered, and you whined and conveniently forgot to do it? Maybe how willing you are depends on the request. Generally, if a parent or a teacher asks for help, your willingness will be appreciated.

But do you need to stop what you're doing and do whatever someone asks whenever you're asked? That's a good question, one you might want to talk about with one of your parents. The important question is, How do you figure out when to help? My mother said deep inside my heart I can find the answer. Maybe you can try this, too.

I will be willing to help others if it feels like the right thing to do.

December 12

Many problems can be avoided.

A problem can be an opportunity to learn an important lesson. Let's say your bike has a flat tire. You noticed the tire was losing air last week, but you were in such a rush to get to Amy's party that you ignored it. Now you're facing the consequences. Pushing the bike to a station for air is not easy on a warm day and could have been avoided.

My foster grandmother has a saying that I like. She says, "Slow your pace if you want to win the race." I didn't get it, but she explained that our rushing around causes mistakes and keeps us from thinking clearly much of the time. This leads to unnecessary failures. Slowing down will give us time to avoid some of life's pitfalls. She says this idea has helped her many times.

My decision to slow down may pay off today.

We usually get what we need.

My friend Stephanie wants to win the state speech contest in the worst way. She has worked hard on her speaking voice. She dropped out of volleyball and often stays after school to practice with the speech coach. I wonder what she'll do if she doesn't win?

My grandmother has this idea that everybody gets what she needs. This doesn't make much sense to me. I don't think I needed my dad to move away last year, but she says another person will come into my life who has important things to teach me. She said that if Stephanie really needs to win the contest, she will. I guess I'll have to wait and see if she's right about these things. What do you believe?

I wonder what I will need today.

December 14

Saying you're sorry can be a broken record.

My friend is constantly saying she's sorry. Often I doubt it. I think she says it just to get out of trouble. Saying you're sorry needs to be sincere. But even more, it needs to indicate that you're willing to be responsible for whatever you did and are determined not to repeat the behavior.

In Girl Scouts, our assignment for the good neighbor badge was to keep a diary of all the times in one week that we had to apologize for our behavior. The second part of the assignment was to list what we should have done instead. I was surprised at how many times I had done things for which I was sorry. My grandmother calls this getting an eye-opener. She says our eye-openers can motivate us to change.

I will be thoughtful today.

We are present for a reason
in one another's lives. Let's pay attention.

Mildred Ebaugh

Have you heard the saying that God doesn't make junk? My mom put this message on my bulletin board. I just noticed it the other day. I don't know when she put it there. She said I wasn't very observant. Anyway, I don't believe it. I think Kitty is junk! She's the new girl in our class, and she's the meanest girl I've ever met. She picks on Reba constantly. Reba is quiet and never says anything back to Kitty. I told Kitty off just last week, and she ignored me. I was furious. She picked on Reba again the next day.

I asked Mom to explain how it could be true that God makes no junk when a person like Kitty is born. She said every person alive is significant in some way. Even Kitty. She asked me to think about what I've learned from knowing Kitty. A person can't be significant and junk at the same time. I've learned a lot from Kitty about what I don't want to be.

I don't want to be thought of as junk.

December 16

Fear can motivate us to change our behavior.

I'm scared. I have a big history test Friday and I haven't even begun to memorize the information Mrs. Holliday gave us about World War II. I didn't do well last grading period, and my parents said if I didn't bring the grade up, I would have to give up track this spring. It will take a miracle for me to get as high a grade as I need to stay on the team.

I'm disgusted with myself. Mom had even said she would quiz me on the information whenever I needed her help. I was always too busy on the phone. I love track and I'm one of the best runners in our school. Not only will I miss out on the meets, I'll be letting my team down. I wonder if I can manage a good grade if I turn all my attention to history for the rest of the week. I will never do this again. Honest!

Why is changing our behavior so hard? Maybe it only seems that way because we don't try.

Who is God?

What picture do you see when you think of God? I see an old man wearing a long white robe. He has a white beard and long white hair. Mom says God doesn't necessarily look like I picture him. She says that none of us will know for sure until we die, but some people believe God looks however each of us pictures him. In other words, when we die we will see God exactly like we pictured God. That's part of the mystery. God can look different to each one of us and still be God.

Aunt Judy believes God is a woman. Uncle Joe says God is man and woman. Lisa believes that the sun and trees represent God. I'm relieved to find out that we can envision God in whatever way we find helpful. Aren't you?

Picturing God today will be fun, especially if I am with a friend who pictures God in a different way.

December 18

Dreams motivate us
to stretch beyond where we are.

Dreams are so much more than short, confusing stories in your mind while you sleep. Dreams are full of information, and you can have a dream wherever you are. Daydreams possibly have more to tell us than other dreams. But all dreams can inform and inspire us. I read that someone like Edison probably had many dreams in his laboratory. Without his dreams, we might still be reading by candlelight.

My dreams might not inspire me to invent something world-changing, but anyone's dreams can change that person's life. My friend Bridget dreams of being a professional dancer. She takes several dance classes a week and is becoming so graceful. Of all my friends, I worried the most about her getting into drugs, but now she cares so much about being in shape and in good health. I think her dream of dancing is shaping her life in a wonderful way.

I will honor my dreams and encourage the dreams of my friends.

A new habit to cultivate is "inner quiet."

Every afternoon my mother takes the phone off the hook and sits and meditates. She has instructed my brother and me to be quiet during that time. We can't ask her any questions and we can't have kids in the house. She says getting quiet inside her heart and mind allows her to feel rested and peaceful. She says she senses what she needs to do next after she has gotten quiet inside.

I might start doing this, too. You don't have to be a certain age. She compared meditating to praying. She said the difference is that when she prays, she talks to God. When she meditates, she listens to her heart. I like it when my mother meditates because our house is so quiet. I wonder what my heart would say to me if I ever stayed quiet enough to listen?

I want to have a way to be peaceful.

December 20

A girl's behavior is the key to her personality.

Do you have a personality that others admire? I wasn't sure about this until my mom pointed out my good qualities. She told me I had a good personality. She said that so many different personalities make the world interesting.

Personality is the combination of our characteristics. One of my good characteristics is that I'm friendly and easy to talk to. My mom says this and so do my friends and their parents. I am gentle with my friends and animals. I'm prompt. I'm never late for school, dinner, the bus, or parties. Mom says being dependable is a great thing.

I can appreciate my own unique personality and other individual personalities.

Learning to compromise helps our friendships.

Jenny can be rude. She walks right into our house without knocking. Sometimes she brings two or three girls with her. I don't like it when she whines about the video I've picked out. I don't like how she acts a lot of the time. Mom said my choice is to accept Jenny like she is or choose another friend.

Is there a friend in your life you enjoy less than before? Mom says that friendship is about learning to compromise if we disagree about what to do. She says that when I have a family of my own and a job, I'll be glad I learned how to compromise. I need to think about what I want to do: practice compromising or choose a new friend.

Today will probably give me an opportunity to compromise.

December 22

We're not too young to learn
what "instant gratification" means.

I read a story last night about a girl who wanted instant gratification. This concept may be new to you. It was new to me. April wanted everything her way and didn't want to wait for it. Her father accused her of wanting instant gratification. She didn't understand. All he said was that she would figure it out someday. I got to figure it out with her.

Here is what happened in the story. April got her allowance one Monday morning like always. On her way to school, she passed the drugstore and saw in the window a small purse with a brush, a comb, a tube of lip balm, and a small bottle of perfume in it. She rushed in and bought it, spending all her allowance. When she got to school, her friends told her they were going to the movies on Saturday, but her money was gone. See how instant gratification can be a bad idea?

Sometimes my reward is sweeter if I wait for it.

What is joy? Do you have it?

At the holiday season, most people seem cheerful. Does giving presents make people happier than they would ordinarily be? Once a week, our principal comes into our classroom for an open discussion. She usually asks us for an idea to discuss. I think joy would be a good topic, particularly since the holidays are near.

I love when I'm asked to spend the afternoon with Penny, the little girl next door. I get paid for watching her. She's so cute and loves to cuddle. Earning money this way makes it possible for me to purchase surprise gifts for my parents. Making them happy when they aren't expecting it is fun.

One thing I've often noticed about feeling joy is that my entire body seems to be light. I like that feeling.

It's possible to find some joy in every day.

December 24

Reacting to one another
before thinking something through
is what causes unnecessary spats.

Linda Reed

When my brother teases me, I'm too quick to get mad. That's what Len, my mom's new boyfriend, says. But I don't think my dad would see it that way. I miss him. He moved away when I was in the third grade. Now I only see him about twice a year because he lives in Texas.

Mom says that Len is just trying to help me see that I don't need to react to Alex. I can ignore him. She says that reacting to him gives him the power to control my life. She called it giving Alex rent-free space in my mind. She learned this the hard way. Her boss used to upset her every day. She dreaded going to work. She finally went to a counselor who told her about the rent-free idea. She said it changed how she felt about everyone. She said I'm not too young to use this idea.

I like the idea of having my mind filled with positive stuff rather than irritations.

Having faith, like having fear, is a choice.

Having faith can make a big difference in how your life turns out. My grandfather told me a story about when he was young. He said his story carried a profound message. His dad died when he was a small boy. His mother took in washing and ironing to make enough money to pay for groceries. Fortunately, they also had a garden. My grandfather had dreamed of becoming a doctor when he grew up, but his mom said she doubted there would be enough money for college. He mentioned this to his teacher one day, and she suggested he study hard, do as much extra credit work as possible, and apply for a scholarship after high school. His mom agreed. She said having faith and working hard could make the difference. For Grandpa it did: he fulfilled his dream and became a doctor.

Do I have enough faith? I want to develop my faith.

December 26

The importance of friendship
should never be underestimated.

Randi Peters

You know what a coincidence is? It's when something happens that you hadn't expected and it ends up being exactly the right thing to have happened. My dad says whatever happens is always some small part of the plan that God has made for our lives.

He said that friends are part of that plan, and our friendships are like the content of books. From them we get the information we need to go on to the next stage in our lives. Without the friend, we wouldn't learn what we need to know. I had always been afraid of heights. My best friend climbs trees like a cat. She "talked me" up a tree. She followed me and told me how to move my hands and feet. I did it. It was a great feeling and a great lesson.

I wonder who will be my teacher today.

Bad habits are like dirty socks.
They need to be traded in for clean ones.

Marie Growe

Bad habits don't just mysteriously appear. I pretend that's the case, especially when I'm getting criticized for one of them. Only yesterday Mom had to remind me for the umpteenth time to put my dishes in the dishwasher after breakfast. I said, as usual, "I can't help it that I forget."

Bad habits get a lot of practice. Good habits are developed in the same way. Is it easier to strengthen the bad ones? Practice of anything is what strengthens it. Mom insists that if I choose one of my good behaviors and practice it regularly, it will become a habit.

I'm working on playing the piano instead of biting my nails.

Today is an opportunity to practice a good habit.

December 28

Are you setting a good example for others to follow?

Do you set a good example? In history class last month we were asked to choose a person from the past hundred years who set a good example for others. The person didn't need to be famous but did need to be worthy of being chosen. I chose my neighbor Mrs. Brown because my classmates had already picked the famous people that came to my mind.

Mrs. Brown is blind. She was in a car accident when she was small. Her dad and her sister were killed. Mrs. Brown's head went through the windshield and her eyes were cut. I think blindness would make me very sad, but Mrs. Brown never seems sad. She's one of the friendliest people I know. I asked her how she stayed so happy, and she said that happiness is a decision a person can make every single day. She said her philosophy is that many things happen to us, and it's what we do with those circumstances that counts. She sets a good example, doesn't she?

I will have the opportunity to be happy
if that's what I want today.

Do you like how you look in the mirror?

When I look in the mirror, I like most of what I see: I like my eyes, my skin, my smile. It's easy to find something I'd like to change, like I wish I had curly hair or weighed ten pounds less. My parents remind me that true beauty comes from inside, from how we live and feel about ourselves from the inside out.

Some people are radiant. They convey warmth and care through their expressions and their personalities. They are attractive, and the attractiveness comes from the expression of their heart. Rather than focusing on the parts of my body I'd like to change, I want to focus on being a better me. How I feel about myself is most important.

I will appreciate who I am, not just how I look.

December 30

Insecurity visits many teenagers.

Most of the time I feel secure in myself as a student and as a soccer player. I feel secure in the love of my family and friends most of the time, too. But sometimes I have insecure moments or days or even weeks. This is when I worry about a test at school, or how I look, or if I can make the soccer team.

My parents say I will feel more secure if I believe that guardian spirits are all around me helping me get through life. Mom says this is how she gets the courage to do all the things she does. Last year she learned how to ride a motorcycle. I asked her if she could see her spirits and she said no, but she was sure they were there. She said there is no other way she could have learned to ride the motorcycle. I should start believing in them.

I will try to get help from my guardian spirits today.

Having faith makes every day of your life easier.

When I was smaller, I was nervous about everything. I was afraid I would get left behind if my family was going to a movie. I worried there wouldn't be enough dessert if I didn't rush through my meal. I was sure that I wouldn't pass the first grade and then the second and so on. Not one of the things I worried about ever happened. Grandma says that's usually the case. We waste a lot of time worrying when we could just leave our lives up to God. She said she does and she's been happy most of her life.

I'm not so sure I know how to leave my life up to God. Do you? Grandma says it means we don't try to force situations to come out a particular way. She said it means being quiet when we're wondering what to do or say when a situation is unfolding. She promises that if I can be really still, I'll feel the direction I need to go in. She has never failed to hear what she needed to hear. But she also said that she had to listen more than a few minutes most of the time.

My faith can give me great happiness today. I will listen.

Index

A

B

C

About the Author

Karen Casey is the author of eleven other books, most recent being *Girls Only!* for seven- to ten-year-old girls. It is a book similar to the one you are holding now.

Her first book, *Each Day a New Beginning*, was published in 1982 and is a book of spiritual meditations for women. It has sold more than three million copies. Eleven of her twelve books are available through Hazelden and in your local bookstores. Ask for them by name: *Worthy of Love*, *The Promise of a New Day* (with Martha Vanceburg), *In God's Care*, *If Only I Could Quit*, *Daily Meditations for Practicing the Course*, *Keepers of the Wisdom*, *A Woman's Spirit*, and *A Life of My Own*.

Karen Casey is a wife, a stepmother, and a grandmother. She splits her time between Florida and Minnesota, and loves to ride her Harley-Davidson motorcycle when she isn't busy at her computer. Her husband, Joe, stays busy building and flying giant-scale radio-controlled airplanes.

HAZELDEN INFORMATION AND EDUCATIONAL SERVICES is a division of the Hazelden Foundation, a not-for-profit organization. Since 1949, Hazelden has been a leader in promoting the dignity and treatment of people afflicted with the disease of chemical dependency.

The mission of the foundation is to improve the quality of life for individuals, families, and communities by providing a national continuum of information, education, and recovery services that are widely accessible; to advance the field through research and training; and to improve our quality and effectiveness through continuous improvement and innovation.

Stemming from that, the mission of this division is to provide quality information and support to people wherever they may be in their personal journey—from education and early intervention, through treatment and recovery, to personal and spiritual growth.

Although our treatment programs do not necessarily use everything Hazelden publishes, our bibliotherapeutic materials support our mission and the Twelve Step philosophy upon which it is based. We encourage your comments and feedback.

The headquarters of the Hazelden Foundation is in Center City, Minnesota. Additional treatment facilities are located in Chicago, Illinois; New York, New York; Plymouth, Minnesota; St. Paul, Minnesota; and West Palm Beach, Florida. At these sites, we provide a continuum of care for men and women of all ages. Our Plymouth facility is designed specifically for youth and families.

For more information on Hazelden, please call 1-800-257-7800. Or you may access our World Wide Web site on the Internet at **www.hazelden.org.**